HIGH-RISK PREGNANCY

IN

HIS HANDS

Daily Devotions During Pregnancy

Sandy Collins, RN, BSN

CreateSpace
Atlanta, GEORGIA

Cover design and images by Natalie Rahberg
www.mycustomartist.com

Copyright © 2016 Sandy Collins

ISBN-13: 978-1536877861
ISBN-10: 1536877867

FOR WOMEN FIGHTING FEAR
AND SEARCHING FOR PEACE
DURING PREGNANCY

AND IN THANKS TO THOSE
WHO SUPPORTED ME

CONTENTS

1st Trimester

2nd Trimester

3rd Trimester

1st Trimester

Week

6

Week 6 Day 1

"Look to the Lord and his strength; seek his face always."
(New International Version, 1 Chron. 16.11)

Praise the Lord! A new life has begun in your womb!
As you begin this difficult journey, I urge you to pursue the
word of God fervently. Pour out your heart to the God who
knows your needs before you even ask. "Trust in him at all
times, O people; pour out your hearts to him, for God is our
refuge. " (Ps. 62.8) He will give you the strength you need. I
pray this Bible study will draw you nearer to your Savior.
May the daily devotions and prayers lift your spirit and
strengthen your faith during this incredible season of your
life.

After finding out we were going to have twins, in
desperation, I asked my husband, "What are we going to do?"
With a reassuring smile he replied, "It'll be fun!"
Unfortunately, I was too terrified of the possible complications
associated with high-risk pregnancies to celebrate fearlessly. I
desperately searched the Bible for reassurance and
encouragement. Thankfully, the God who created the
universe revealed to me that He was shaping my unborn
children with His very own hands. Once I understood that
nothing outside of His design could occur, I began to rejoice in
the journey. Nothing could change the peace that came with
surrendering to God's divine will for our lives.

"For I know the plans I have for you," declares the Lord,
"plans to prosper you and not to harm you, plans to give you
hope and a future. Then you will call upon me and come and
pray to me, and I will listen to you. You will seek me and find
me when you seek me with all your heart." (Jer. 29.11-13)

Prayer

Heavenly Father,

I come before You rejoicing for the gift of life You have bestowed upon me. Grant me faith to trust in Your holy will and courage to celebrate this moment. Please allow the words in this devotional to encourage me throughout my pregnancy. In Jesus' name, amen.

Song

MercyMe. "Word of God Speak." *Spoken For*. Provident Music Distribution, 2002. CD.

Week 6 Day 2

"Remember the wonders he has done, his miracles, and the judgments he pronounced..." (1 Chron.16.12)

Right now there is a tiny and amazing miracle growing inside of you. Your baby's heart is already beating! His eyes and ears are beginning to form and his brain even has five distinct areas. The tissue needed to make your child's bones is growing, as well as tiny arm and leg buds. (U.S. National Library of Medicine, Web.) The same God who fashioned the world out of darkness has created an incredible, little person within your womb! Take some time today to ponder this miracle and praise the Lord.

His Creation
With Your words You brought light into the darkness,
And formed the land upon the sea.
You let the stars shine farthest,
Reaching still to me.
As I stroll through the garden and meadows,
Where trees and flowers bloom,
Vibrant colors echo,
"He will return soon!"
The diverse design of all of Your creatures
Is evidence of Your glory.
You created beauty in this earth,
To tell Your love story.
When I observe the wonders of this earth,
I'm humbled by Your plan.
For I await a birth
Formed by Your own hand!
-Sandy Collins

Prayer

Dear God, Maker of Heaven and of Earth,

Thank You for the beautiful world I live in and the mercy You have shown me. Please grant special protection to my little one and keep my heart steadfast. In Jesus' name, amen.

Song

Tomlin, Chris, and Steven Curtis. Chapman. "Indescribable." *Arriving*. Sparrow, 2004. CD.

Week 6 Day 3

"Sons are a heritage from the Lord, children a reward from him. Like arrows in the hands of a warrior are sons born in one's youth. Blessed is the man whose quiver is full of them." (Ps. 127.3-5)

Sometimes an unexpected or multiple pregnancy can feel overwhelming and frightening. My husband and I were astonished when we learned I was carrying two babies. In fact, up until that point, we had it all planned out. We had already chosen a name, planned the bedroom accommodations and selected slim-lined car seats to avoid a mini-van. After my initial sonogram, we stayed in a preoccupied state of perplexed joy and fear for about a week. I was consumed with worry over the increased domestic responsibilities and complications, while my husband contemplated the logistics of having twins.

I truly wish I would have had a devotional book dedicated to helping me walk through that amazing and difficult season of my life. I needed someone to help me find peace in God's sovereignty and faithfulness.

"The Lord himself goes before you and will be with you; he will never leave you nor forsake you. Do not be afraid; do not be discouraged." (Deut. 31.8)

"Nothing is or can be accidental with God."
-Henry Wadsworth Longfellow

Prayer

Dear Heavenly Father,

I am apprehensive about this pregnancy. Please surround me with Your love and mercy. Grant in me a pure heart that seeks to live according to Your will. Give me courage to face the coming days through the promise of Your presence and love for us. Help me to rejoice in the blessing of Your creation and the gift of motherhood. In Jesus' name, amen.

Song

Casting Crowns. "Already There." *Come to the Well*. Integrity Media, 2011. CD

Week 6 Day 4

"The angel went to her and said, "Greetings, you who are highly favored! The Lord is with you." Mary was greatly troubled at his words and wondered what kind of greeting this might be. But the angel said to her, "Do not be afraid, Mary, you have found favor with God. You will be with child and give birth to a son, and you are to give him the name Jesus..." (Luke 1.28-31) "I am the Lord's servant," Mary answered. "May it be to me as you have said." Then the angel left her." (Luke 1.38)

Can you imagine how the Virgin Mary felt when the angel of the Lord told her she would give birth to the Savior? Certainly she was frightened for the angel said, "Do not be afraid, Mary, you have found favor with God." Even though her pregnancy was potentially shameful, Mary chose to accept God's plan with grace. She knew she needed a Savior and she was willing to trust in God's design.

Praise the Lord for you also have been blessed! God has chosen to make you a mother to this unborn child. Perhaps, you are uncomfortable with the complications associated with your pregnancy. Your Heavenly Father is willing and able to transform your heart and bestow upon you every gift and ability necessary to accomplish His purpose. He is waiting for you to open your heart and surrender to Him.

Prayer

Dear Lord,

I place my life and my future in Your hands. Help me to embrace Your plan with confidence and joy. For You, O God, are faithful. Please watch over the tiny miracle growing within me. In Jesus' name, amen.

Song

Grant, Amy. "Breath of Heaven." *Home For Christmas*. A&M Records, 1992. CD.

Week 6 Day 5

"Come and see what God has done, how awesome his works in man's behalf." (Ps. 66.5)

Have you told anyone the news yet? Perhaps you are eager to tell the world your wonderful news or maybe you are more inclined to cherish these days quietly. Either way, thankfully acknowledge God's marvelous gift of creation.

This is Mary's song when she told her cousin, Elizabeth, her incredible news. (Luke 1.46-55)

My soul glorifies the Lord
And my spirit rejoices in God my Savior,
For he has been mindful
Of the humble state of his servant.
From now on all generations will call me blessed,
For the Mighty One has done great things for me-holy is his name.
His mercy extends to those who fear him,
From generation to generation.
He has performed mighty deeds with his arm;
He has scattered those who are proud in their inmost thoughts.
He has brought down rulers from their thrones
But has lifted up the humble.
He has filled the hungry with good things
But has sent the rich away empty.
He has helped his servant Israel,
Remembering to be merciful
To Abraham and his descendants forever,
Even as he said to our fathers.

God is faithful and He always remembers you. He assures you He will never leave you, nor forsake you. So rejoice, mother to be, and let your soul glorify the Lord!

Prayer

Lord,

I praise You for the amazing works You have done and I look forward to the fulfillment of all the promises You have made. Please bless this child and keep me ever mindful of Your unwavering love. In Jesus' name, amen.

Song

Downhere. "How Many Kings." *Ending is Beginning*. Centricity Music, 2008. CD.

Week 7 Day 1

"Are not two sparrows sold for a penny? Yet not one of them will fall to the ground apart from the will of your Father. And even the very hairs of your head are all numbered. So don't be afraid; you are worth more than many sparrows." (Matt. 10.29-30)

When I see a flock of birds soaring through the sky it amazes me that God remembers each one. Even more so, when I contemplate the vast number of people of whom God is simultaneously aware. I am humbled because I know He is still mindful of me. All I have to do is whisper a prayer in my heart, and I know I have been heard. Can you remember a time when you were fully aware of God's immediate concern for you?

Once I took my child to an urgent care facility to receive treatment for a laceration on his palm. My interaction with the staff was terribly frustrating, and I felt helpless as my young son screamed from the unnecessary pain being inflicted. Exasperated, I internally cried out, "Please help me, God!" No sooner had I finished my prayer, then a competent and capable nurse entered the room. She calmly intervened and changed the entire outcome of the situation. God sent her to answer my desperate prayer immediately and even before my words had ended. I knew then that God cares for each of in us every moment of every day, even more than the sparrows.

Prayer
Dearest Jesus,
     Thank you for remembering me and caring about my every need. Please guard and protect my sweet baby until the day comes for me to meet her. Amen.

Song
Hill, Lauryn. "His Eye is on the Sparrow." *Sister Act 2: Back in the Habit.* Hollywood Records, 1993. CD.

Week 7 Day 2

"Sarah said, "God has brought me laughter, and everyone who hears about this will laugh with me." And she added, "Who would have said to Abraham that Sarah would nurse children? Yet I have borne him a son in his old age." (Gen. 21.6)

Can you envision Sarah giving birth to Isaac at 90 years old? Isaac, Sarah's only child, was the fulfillment of God's promise to Abraham 25 years before. God had determined that Abraham would be the father of many nations. However, Sarah grew weary of waiting for the divine blessing and attempted to manipulate God's will by coercing Abraham to produce an heir with her maidservant. Ultimately, God fulfilled His promise through Abraham and Sarah's legitimate son, Isaac, in His own time.

If you have been classified as being of advanced maternal age, remember that God is not impeded by our human expectations or aging bodies. "Is anything too hard for the Lord?" (Gen. 18.13) God still works miracles and your baby is part of His plan.

Prayer
Dearest Savior,

Thank You for the gracious blessing of a child. Help me to trust in Your plan and rejoice in Your timing. You are good, Lord, and I praise You. Forgive me when I am consumed by my own will and not Yours. Amen.

Song
Hall, Mark. "Who But You." *Music Inspired by the Story*. Capitol Christian Music Group, 2011. CD.

Week 7 Day 3

"Now the Lord was gracious to Sarah as he had said, and the Lord did for Sarah what he had promised. Sarah became pregnant and bore a son to Abraham in his old age, at the very time God had promised him." (Gen. 21.1-2)

It is often very difficult to wait for God's will. However, when we look back at our lives, we can see evidence of God's design. What wonderful and unexpected blessings have happened in your life? In Ravi Zacharias' book, *The Grand Weaver*, Zacharias describes how a father and son create some of the most beautiful wedding saris in the world. An Indian wedding sari is a long garment made of cotton or silk that is draped across the body and over the head of women in an elegant fashion.

"…the father sat above the son on a platform, surrounded by several spools of thread that he would gather in to his fingers. The son had only one task. At the nod of his father, he would move the shuttle from one side to the other and back again. This would then be repeated for hundreds of hours, until a magnificent pattern began to emerge. The son certainly had the easier task. He was only to move at the father's nod. But making use of these efforts, the father was working to an intricate end. All along, he had the design in his mind and was bringing the right threads together."

You may not always perceive the extraordinary masterpiece God is creating with the pieces of your life, but rest assured, His works are wonderful.

Prayer

Dear Heavenly Father,

Give me the wisdom to see Your hand pulling together the pieces of my life and open my eyes to the beauty of Your divine design. In Jesus' name, Amen.

Song

Wickham, Phil. "Glory." *The Ascension*. Fair Trade Services, 2013. CD.

Week 7 Day 4

"Sarah said, "God has brought me laughter, and everyone who hears about this will laugh with me." (Gen. 21.6)

Indeed, Sarah was surprised to see the promise fulfilled after her childbearing years had already passed. But Sarah and Abraham's joy was most evident when they named their child Isaac, which means "laughter." Through the miraculous conception and birth of Isaac, the glory and power of God was revealed to all the world.

Naturally, your baby will bring you many moments of laughter and some times of tears. Remember that through them all God is always near.

"Joy is the echo of God's life within us."
-Joseph Marmion

Prayer
Amazing God,

I know You desire that all people be saved. You use miracles and circumstances to turn people's hearts toward You. Help me to focus on You. Thank You for the joy this child brings and the laughter that I will one day hear. May my heart rejoice and praise You. In Jesus' name, amen.

Song
Card, Michael. "They Call Him Laughter." *Ancient Faith Box Set*. Sparrow, 1993. CD.

Week 7 Day 5

"Before I formed you in the womb I knew you, before you were born I set you apart..." (Jer. 1.5)

The desire to be known and to be loved for who you are is at the very essence of a person's being. Perhaps, that is why God is saying, "Before I formed you...I knew you..." With those words God reassures you of His unconditional love. He chose the color of your hair, the shape of your smile, and the very talents you possess. He delights in you, for you are the work of His own hands. You have been set apart for a specific role as mother to the masterpiece within you. God has purposefully and lovingly created your child to be part of His divine plan as well. He knows your child by name and is pleased with the individual characteristics he has been given. What a wonderful day it will be when you see your baby, God's unique creation, for the first time!

Prayer

Dear Creator God,

Thank You for making this tiny gift within me and allowing me to be his mother. I rejoice in the gift of life, the promise of Your presence and Your faithful guidance. Please watch over my child as he continues to develop. Help me to love and nurture Your darling masterpiece. In Jesus' name, amen.

Song

Patty, Sandi. "Masterpiece" *A Mother's Prayer*. Word Entertainment LLC, 2008. CD.

Week 8 Day 1

"He settles the barren woman in her home as a happy mother of children. Praise the Lord." (Ps. 113.9)

The Bible is filled with stories of women to whom God graciously granted children. God blessed Sarah, Rebekah, Rachel, and Hannah with the birth of a baby after years of disappointment and sorrow.

Now, it is your turn to rejoice in the gift God has given you. At 8 weeks old your child's hands, feet, and lungs are beginning to form. Her arms and legs are getting longer, while her brain is continuing to grow and develop. (U.S. National Library of Medicine, Web)

May God bless the child within you. Give thanks to the Lord for He is good! His mercy endures forever.

Prayer

Dear Jesus,

You have taken away my despair and given me hope. I will praise You with all of my heart. Thank You for the kindness You have shown me. Bless my child and strengthen my womb so that if it be Your will, I may bring forth a beautiful, vibrant infant. Amen.

Song

Tomlin, Chris. "Jesus Loves Me." *Love Ran Red*. Sparrow Records, 2014. CD.

Week 8 Day 2

"And the Lord was gracious to Hannah; she conceived and gave birth to three sons and two daughters. Meanwhile, the boy Samuel grew up in the presence of the Lord."
(1 Sam. 2.21)

Hannah was the wife of Elkanah and had no children. She was very grieved by her barrenness and begged God to grant her a son. While fervently praying in the temple, Hannah pledged to give the child to God for all his days if God would bless her with a baby. After returning home from their trip to the temple "…the Lord remembered her. So in the course of time Hannah conceived and gave birth to a son. She named him Samuel, saying, `Because I asked the Lord for him.'" (1 Sam. 1.20)

Just like Hannah, you are in God's thoughts and He has been gracious to you. He has given you this child and now you must ensure that "…as for me and my household, we will serve the Lord." (Josh. 24.15) Hannah fulfilled her promise and gave Samuel to be a helper in the temple of the Lord. Eventually, Samuel became a great prophet for God.

God instructs parents to "Train a child in the way he should go, and when he is old he will not turn from it." (Prov. 22.6) This will be your most important responsibility as a mother. You must pass on the truth you know in your heart. "For God so loved the world that he gave his one and only Son, that whosoever believes in him shall not perish but have eternal life." (John 3.16)

Prayer

Gracious Heavenly Father,

Thank You for remembering me and blessing me with this child. Give me the wisdom I need to teach my child about You so that we may spend eternity together. In Jesus' name, Amen.

Song

Story, Laura. "Blessings." *Blessings*. Fair Trade Services, 2011.CD.

Week 8 Day 3

"I prayed for this child, and the Lord has granted me what I asked of him. So now I give him to the Lord. For his whole life he will be given over to the Lord." And he worshiped the Lord there." (1 Sam. 1.27)

Hannah's Prayer

"My heart rejoices in the Lord;
In the Lord my horn is lifted high.
My mouth boasts over my enemies,
For I delight in your deliverance.
"There is no one holy like the Lord;
There is no one besides you;
There is no Rock like our God.
"Do not keep talking so proudly
Or let your mouth speak such arrogance,
For the Lord is a God who knows,
And by him deeds are weighed.
"The bows of the warriors are broken,
But those who stumbled are armed with strength.
Those who were full hire themselves out for food,
But those who were hungry hunger no more.
She who was barren has borne seven children,
But she who has had many sons pines away.
"The Lord brings death and makes alive;
He brings down to the grave and raises up.
The Lord sends poverty and wealth;
He humbles and he exalts.
He raises the poor from the dust
And lifts the needy from the ash heap;
He seats them with princes
And has them inherit a throne of honor.

"For the foundations of the earth are the Lord's;
Upon them he has set the world.
He will guard the feet of his saints,
But the wicked will be silenced in darkness.
"It is not by strength that one prevails;
Those who oppose the Lord will be shattered.
He will thunder against them from heaven;
The Lord will judge the ends of the earth.
"He will give strength to his king
And exalt the horn of his anointed.'"
(1 Sam. 2.1-10)

Hannah's song of praise is devoted to the God who lifted her up to a position of honor. The inability of a woman to produce a child during Hannah's lifetime was not only devastating, but shameful. Hannah's life was completely transformed by the sovereign power of God. Are you mindful of God's loving hand touching your life? In a matter of weeks, you will see one of His most incredible wonders growing and moving within you. Therefore, praise the Lord and sing of His goodness!

Prayer
Sovereign Lord,
I praise You for the amazing things You have done and I thank You for this child. Let me always remember that Your ways are wonderful. In Jesus' name, amen.

Song
Tomlin, Chris. "Holy is Lord." *Sacred Revolution: Songs from One Day 03*. Six Steps Records, 2003.CD.

Week 8 Day 4

"Each year his mother made him a little robe and took it to him when she went up with her husband to offer the annual sacrifice. Eli would bless Elkanah and his wife, saying, "May the Lord give you children by this woman to take the place of the one she prayed for and gave to the Lord." Then they would go home. And the Lord was gracious to Hannah; she conceived and gave birth to three sons and two daughters. Meanwhile, the boy Samuel grew up in the presence of the Lord." (1 Sam. 2.19-21)

What must Hannah have felt during her annual visit with her son? Did she regret her vow to God or was she still thankful enough to offer up her treasured child without reservations? Did she wonder how any other child could take the place of Samuel as Eli prayed?

I was devastated when we lost our second child. I was angry, ashamed, hurt, and even frightened. How could any child replace the one we had lost? He can't, but another child can bring astonishing joy to life. After much time, I am beginning to comprehend the greater design God had in mind. He was not punishing me or abandoning me. That experience helped equip me to comfort others who are suffering. I rejoice in the children God has chosen to bless my earthly life with because I know He is holding the child we lost.

Prayer
Lord,

You are the giver of all good things. Thank You for filling my life with unexpected and wonderful blessings. Forgive me when I fail to trust in Your almighty wisdom. Give me faith to always follow You. In Jesus' name, amen.

Song
Wickham, Phil. "This Is Amazing Grace." *The Ascension*. Fair Trade Services, 2013. CD.

Week 8 Day 5

"...Then Eli said, He is the Lord; let him do what is good in his eyes." (1 Sam. 3.18)

In this Bible story concerning Eli and his wicked sons, God's judgment is severe. However, I want to focus on Eli's attitude. He humbled himself before the Lord and surrendered willingly to God's righteous decision. Are you able to accept God's will as holy? Letting go of your control over life can be frightening unless you fully comprehend how much God loves you. "Yet the Lord longs to be gracious to you; he rises to show you compassion. For the Lord is a God of justice. Blessed are all who wait for him!" (Isa. 30.18)

"To walk out of God's will is to step into nowhere."
- C.S. Lewis

Prayer
Lord of Compassion,
        Thank You for seeing me through Your eyes of mercy and love. Lead me in the ways of Your righteousness. I place my life and the life of my child into Your hands. Trusting in Your mercy, I pray. In Jesus' name, amen.

Song
Casting Crowns. "Praise You in this Storm." *Lifesong*. Reunion Records, 2005. CD.

Week 9 Day 1

"You turned my wailing into dancing; you removed my sackcloth and clothed me with joy, my heart may sing to you and not be silent. O my god, I will give you thanks forever." (Ps. 30.11-12)

During this first trimester, when morning sickness is often agonizing, remember this is a temporary condition that requires a tremendous amount of energy. Rest assured, this discomfort will be worthwhile when you finally hold your newborn child. For now, it is important to be purposeful in giving thanks to God for the child developing inside of you and the hormones causing your discomfort, but also maintaining your pregnancy.

At this moment, your child has already grown elbows and toes! Every major organ has begun to develop, along with hair follicles and nipples. (U.S. National Library of Medicine, Web)

Praise God joyfully for filling your life with great expectations even in the midst of your discomfort. "Be joyful always; pray continually; give thanks in all circumstances, for this is God's will for you in Christ Jesus." (1 Thess. 5.16-18)

Prayer
Dear Jesus,

Please sustain me during this difficult time. I am grateful for this child, but I am feeling very ill. Strengthen me by Your power and give me the rest I need to help this baby thrive. Thank You for Your goodness. In Jesus' name, amen.

Song
Kutless. "We Fall Down." *Strong Tower*. BEC Recordings, 2005. CD.

Week 9 Day 2
"Now when Daniel learned that the decree had been published, he went home to his upstairs room where the windows opened toward Jerusalem. Three times a day he got down on his knees and prayed, giving thanks to his God, just as he had done before. Then these men went as a group and found Daniel praying and asking God for help. So they went to the king and spoke to him about his royal decree..." (Dan. 6.10-12)

When you found out you were in the "high-risk" pregnancy category did you run to your Savior like Daniel? Even with the threat of death, Daniel sought out the Lord in prayer, just as he had always done. Daniel understood that in the midst of great trials we need God's help. I encourage you to seek the Lord when you are facing insurmountable circumstances. God is not intimidated by your worldly problems because He has already overcome death, the grave and the troubles of this world.

Prayer
Almighty God,
I know You have conquered death and that You understand the trials I face. I pray that if it is Your will, You will save me from these challenging times. According to Your will, make my child healthy and strong. Let him grow safely in my womb. In Jesus' name, amen.

Song
Hillsong United. "Touch the Sky." *Empires*. Hillsong Music Australia, 2015. CD.

Week 9 Day 3

"So the king gave the order, and they brought Daniel and threw him into the lions' den. The king said to Daniel, "May your God, whom you serve continually, rescue you!"...The king was overjoyed and gave orders to lift Daniel out of the den. And when Daniel was lifted from the den, no wound was found on him, because he had trusted in his God." (Dan. 6.16-22)

Daniel was a champion of faith. He trusted God to save him even when the world turned against him. During his life Daniel sought to serve the Lord faithfully in word and deed. God rewarded him for his faithfulness by saving him from the mouths of lions.

I believe God still rewards those who are faithful for it says in the Matthew, "His master replied, 'Well done, good and faithful servant! You have been faithful with a few things; I will put you in charge of many things. Come and share your master's happiness!" (Matt. 25.21) God gives you opportunities to trust Him and to follow where He leads. May the Lord bless you and your baby as you continue to abide in His great love.

Prayer
Dear Jesus,
Thank You for the stories of Your faithful servants in the Bible. Help me be faithful and to trust in You unswervingly through life's trials. Amen.

Song
Daigle, Lauren. "Trust In You." *How Can It Be*. Centricity Music, 2015. CD.

Week 9 Day 4

"Then King Darius wrote to all the peoples, nations and men of every language throughout the land: "May you prosper greatly! "I issue a decree that in every part of my kingdom people must fear and reverence the God of Daniel. "For he is the living God and he endures forever; his kingdom will not be destroyed, his dominion will never end. He rescues and he saves; he performs signs and wonders in the heavens and on the earth. He has rescued Daniel from the power of the lions." (Dan. 6.25-27)

Here it is! This is evidence that God can work through difficult circumstances to bring glory to His kingdom. Through Daniel's frightening trial in the lions' den, God was able to move the heart of King Dairus to profess that God is the "...living God and he endures forever; his kingdom will not be destroyed, his dominion will never end. He rescues and he saves; he performs signs and wonders in the heavens and on the earth..." to his entire kingdom! Daniel's faithfulness had a profound impact on the lives of those around him. How will your faith story influence people in your life?

Prayer
Dear Lord,
Help me to live my life in a way that testifies to Your great love. Please watch over my baby and help me to lead him to Your saving light. In Jesus' name. Amen.

Song
The Afters. "Light Up the Sky." *Light Up the Sky*. Fair Trade Services, 2010. CD.

Week 9 Day 5

"Forget the former things; do not dwell on the past. See, I am doing a new thing! Now it springs up; do you not perceive it? I am making a way in the desert." (Isa. 43.18-19)

I remember my husband asking me, "When are you going to be happy about this baby?" I was already several weeks into my pregnancy, but I had miscarried the previous child. In anger I replied, "When it's born!" What an awful reflection of the fear consuming me. I wish someone had spoken the words of Isaiah 43 over me. Then my heart could have rejoiced sooner about our unborn daughter. If you are overwhelmed with anxiety about this pregnancy because of a previous loss, "...do not dwell on the past. See, I am doing a new thing!" Let your heart be glad and celebrate this moment. This is a new beginning. May God bless you and your child throughout your pregnancy with His loving presence and peace.

Prayer
Dear Jesus,
Help me to rejoice over the new life within me with. Walk with me on this journey and surround us with Your love and mercy. Give me the faith I need to trust in You so that my heart may be filled with joy and hope. Amen.

Song
Gokey, Danny. "Tell Your Heart to Beat Again." *Hope In Front Of Me.* BMG Rights Management, 2014. CD.

Week 10 Day 1

"This is the day the Lord has made; let us rejoice and be glad in it." (Ps. 118.24)

It is tempting to wish away difficult days and problems, but God can use those moments to shape us into the person He wants us to be. He can use bed rest to teach us patience, perseverance, hope, and contentment. Conflicts turn us back toward our Savior and often help us articulate our faith. Sorrows will draw us nearer to our Great Comforter and fellow believers. Whatever the circumstance, we are to rejoice because we have joy in the knowledge of our eternal salvation. So let us find happiness in everyday for "This is the day the Lord has made..."

Prayer
Dear Lord,
Thank You for another day and the chance to see Your hand in it. Let me praise You every day of my life as I seek to find happiness in the time You've given me. Thank You for protecting my child and me each day. In Jesus' name, amen.

Song
Redman, Matt. "10,000 Reasons."10,000 Reasons. Six Step Records, 2012. CD.

Week 10 Day 2

"Her husband has full confidence in her and lacks nothing of value. She brings him good, not harm, all the days of her life." (Prov. 31.11-12)

Sometimes it is easy to be consumed with your own feelings and experiences when you are pregnant. After all, you are the one carrying the baby! However, this pregnancy is an exciting, and sometimes intimidating, transition for your husband as well. Have you spoken openly and respectfully to your spouse about this pregnancy? What kind of expectations and fears does he have? How can you bring him good right now? You are your husband's crown, his pride, and his joy. Soon, you will be the mother of his child. You are imperative to his success and happiness. Men often feel responsible for a woman's emotional well-being. Consequently, when you are content it is easier for him to be glad.

Together you have the opportunity to build a family centered on Christ for "Though one may be overpowered, two can defend themselves. A cord of three strands is not quickly broken." (Eccles. 4.12)

Prayer
Dear Heavenly Father,

Thank you for my husband and for our family. Help me to support my dearest love all of my life. Keep our home grounded on Your truth and promises so that we may walk in faith. In Jesus' name, amen.

Song
Smith, Michael. "Forever Yours." *Wonder.* Reunion Records, 2010. CD.

Week 10 Day 3

"Bear with each other and forgive whatever grievances you may have against one another. Forgive as the Lord forgave you. And over all these virtues put on love, which binds them all together in perfect unity." (Col. 3.13-14)

Have you been offended? Has a friend, family member, or even a stranger spoken hurtful or cruel words about you or your pregnancy? It's an awful feeling and if you're like me, you replay the incident in your head repeatedly to determine what you should have said or done in response. Although some contemplation is reasonable, dwelling on negative experiences and lingering in unforgiveness is harmful. I truly believe that is why God commands us to forgive. When we are free from hate and vengeful feelings, we can be filled with God's Holy Spirit instead.

Have you ever said anything you regret? I read once that the best solution is to immediately say, "I'm sorry." when you realize you have misspoken. God has forgiven you and me for our countless trespasses of the tongue and heart. He graciously welcomes us back because He is faithful. Therefore, how much more should we forgive those who have sinned against us? It is not easy to forgive unkind words, but it is necessary. Some comments deserve reasonable reflection, but others should not be allowed to crush your spirit. May God give you a discerning heart to distinguish between them.

Prayer

Dear Lord,

Help me to forgive the unkind words and sentiment of those who cause me pain. Please forgive me when I fail to speak words that build others up. Wrap me in Your love and cleanse me from my sins. In Jesus' name, amen.

Song

Casting Crowns. "East to West." *The Altar and the Door.* Reunion Records, 2007. CD.

Week 10 Day 4

"It was he who gave some to be apostles, some to be prophets, some to be evangelists, and some to be pastors and teachers, to prepare God's people for works of service, so that the body of Christ may be built up until we all reach unity in the faith and in the knowledge of the Son of God and become mature, attaining to the whole measure of the fullness of Christ." (Eph. 4.11-13)

I believe we all search for meaning in our life. It took me a long time to understand that my worth and contribution to this world was defined by my identity in Christ. We are royalty, children of the King. Therefore, we will inherit the kingdom of God! Our purpose is to serve God and to help others know Jesus using our unique, God-given talents. God has chosen you to lead your child to faith and to love the Lord with all his heart. This may be the most important work you will ever do. May God bless you as you faithfully carry out the tasks He has prepared for you.

Prayer
Lord,
I am so thankful to be part of the body of Christ. Please help me use my talents to serve You and to lead my child to faith. May we both enjoy a close relationship with You. Watch over my baby as he grows. In Jesus' name, amen.

Song
Unspoken. "Lift My Life Up." *Unspoken*. Centricity Music, 2014. CD.

Week 10 Day 5

"Restore us, O God; make your face shine upon us, that we may be saved." (Ps. 80.3)

At 10 weeks, the facial features of your child become more distinct and she has eyelids that have begun to close. Soon, you will be able to recognize your baby because of her individual appearance. She will be set apart as yours from her first day in the nursery. You won't need an arm bracelet to identify your baby because her face will be forever etched in your heart.

During a very difficult time in my life, I attended church simply for the blessing that was spoken over the congregation at the end of every service. "The Lord bless you and keep you; the Lord make his face shine upon you and be gracious to you; the Lord turn his face toward you and give you peace." (Num. 6.24-27) I was seeking the peace only He could give because I knew, even then, that He was the source of all my blessings.

May the Lord's face shine upon you, dear woman.

Prayer

Dearest Savior,

Look upon me, Your child, and restore me. Save me from my sins and keep my heart steadfast. Turn Your face toward me, Lord, for I know You are the giver of all good things. Please bless my child and me, as I carry her. Amen.

Song

West, Matthew. "More." *Happy*. Sparrow Records, 2003. CD.

Week 11 Day 1

"By faith Abraham, when God tested him, offered Isaac as a sacrifice. He who had received the promises was about to sacrifice his one and only son, even though God had said to him, "It is through Isaac that your offspring will be reckoned." Abraham reasoned that God could raise the dead, and figuratively speaking, he did receive Isaac back from death." (Heb. 11.17-19)

Ever since I was a child, this story was very disturbing to me. Until, I understood that Abraham believed God could raise Isaac from the dead. Abraham did not view his actions as murder because he trusted God to restore Isaac to life. God was testing Abraham's faithfulness and his ability to follow Him at all costs.

Sometimes, mothers and fathers don't get to enjoy a lifetime of memories with their children. When that happens, we as parents can take comfort in the knowledge that God will one day restore life to the children we lost. We will see them with a new body on resurrection day and we will spend eternity in heaven together.

Prayers
Dear Jesus,

I pray that you would grant my child life eternal with You. Create a living faith in his heart and if it be Your will, let me share a lifetime with him. Thank You for the gift of life and the promise of our salvation. Amen.

Song
Sidewalk Prophets."Help Me Find It." *Live Like That.* Word Entertainment, 2012. CD.

Week 11 Day 2

"Then I said to you, "Do not be terrified; do not be afraid of them. The Lord your God, who is going before you, will fight for you, as he did for you in Egypt, before your very eyes, and in the desert. There you saw how the Lord your God carried you, as a father carries his son, all the way you went until you reached this place." (Deut. 1.29-31)

Remember the incredible stories of God rescuing the Israelites from slavery in Egypt? The miracles God performed were a magnificent testimony to the power of our Almighty God. When the Israelites were fleeing from Egypt, God parted the Red Sea so they could cross on dry land. That is how great His concern was and is for His children. He goes before you on this journey to prepare a way for you. God is faithful, and He will be with you during this challenging pregnancy. So do not be afraid of the future because God is already there.

Prayer
Dear Heavenly Father,
Help me to boldly embrace the future because I know You are already there. Keep my child and me in Your loving grasp. Forgive me for my doubting heart. Thank You for giving me the stories in the Bible to remind me of Your faithfulness through all the ages. In Jesus' name, amen.

Song
Kutless. "What Faith Can Do." *It Is Well*. BEC Recordings, 2009. CD.

Week 11 Day 3

"Even the sparrow has found a home, and the swallow a nest for herself, where she may have her young-a place near your altar, O Lord Almighty, my King and my God. Blessed are those who dwell in your house; they are ever praising you. Blessed are those whose strength is in you, who have set their hearts on pilgrimages. As they pass through the Valley of Baca, they make it a place of springs; the autumn rains also cover it with pools." (Ps. 84.3-6)

I encourage you to prayerfully seek a church home where you can joyfully build your nest to worship near God's altar. When you're searching, or if you feel frustrated with your church, remember that no organization is perfect. Churches are filled with God's imperfect people and God bids us to love one another and to forgive each other. A church family can help support you through some of life's most difficult challenges and joyful celebrations.

If you are on restricted activity, take heart because the verse for today also says, "As they pass through the Valley of Baca, they make it a place of springs..." The Valley of Baca is referring to "...arid stretches the pilgrims had to transverse..." (New International Version Concordance, 875). The pilgrims' hopeful expectations helped "...transform difficult ways into places of refreshment..." God has given you His word and the fellowship of other believers to help you prevail with hopeful anticipation. May your Christian friends uplift you in prayer and with their presence.

Prayer

Dear Heavenly Father,

Thank You for watching over all Your children, especially me. Please help us find a place to worship You and to fellowship with other believers. Strengthen my heart with Your promises and guard my precious child. Please surround me with other believers who will transform this time into a time of refreshment. In Jesus' name, amen.

Song

Tenth Avenue North. "No Man Is an Island." *Cathedrals*. Provident Label Group, 2014. CD.

Week 11 Day 4

"Isaac prayed to the Lord on behalf of his wife, because she was barren. The Lord answered his prayer, and his wife Rebekah became pregnant. The babies jostled each other within her, and she said, "Why is this happening to me?" So she went to inquire of the Lord. The Lord said to her, "Two nations are in your womb, and two peoples from within you will be separated; one people will be stronger than the other, and the older will serve the younger." (Gen. 25.21-23)

I have always been touched by the love story of Isaac and Rebekah. From the first day they met, "...he loved her; and Isaac was comforted after his mother's death." (Gen. 24.67) Surely, as Abraham and Sarah's child, Isaac must have heard the story of his own miraculous birth in fulfillment of God's promise. Is that why he prayerfully intervened on behalf of his beloved wife? Isaac must have believed that the God who had promised to make his father's descendants as numerous as the stars would hear his prayers. God willingly granted Isaac's request and also comforted Rebekah with an explanation for the struggle inside her womb. God's love for Rebekah and His faithfulness is evident throughout this story. When has God demonstrated His love for you? It is good to be thankful for the blessings God has bestowed upon you, especially your spouse.

"Love is a command, not just a feeling. Somehow, in the romantic world of music and theater we have made love to be what it is not. We have so mixed it with beauty and charm and sensuality and contact that we have robbed it of its higher call of cherishing and nurturing."
(Zacharias, I, Isaac, 39)

Prayer

Dear Heavenly Father,

Thank You for listening to all my prayers. Help me to listen and to wait for Your reply. Let me always trust in Your unfailing love and promises. Thank You for my husband and for the life we share together. Let us seek You always as we build our family. In Jesus' name, amen.

Song

Chapman, Steven. "I Will Be Here." *More to This Life*. Capitol Records, 1989. CD.

Week 11 Day 5

"Do not let your hearts be troubled. Trust in God; trust also in me. In my Father's house are many rooms; if it were not so, I would not have told you. And if I go and prepare a place for you, I will come back and take you to be with me that you also may be where I am. You know the way to the place I am going." (John 14.1-4)

Our second oldest child was induced early due to complications. As I lay in the hospital bed after an external cephalic version, where the doctor turned my child from a breech position to a head-down position, the doctor announced, "This baby is coming today!" I broke down in tears and cried out, "But I'm not ready!" We had moved from out of state less than two weeks before and many boxes were still unopened. Nothing was ready! What were we going to do? The procedure was only supposed to prepare me for labor later that month, not that same day!

Surprises are a part of life. Sometimes, they are a welcome blessing and other instances present challenges that enable us to grow stronger in our faith. As we reflect on God's faithfulness during our lifetime, we can see evidence of His great love. God already knows our needs before we even ask, yet He longs for us to present our requests to Him. He is bigger than your need, and He loves you.

I was deeply moved when we arrived home to a completely unpacked, organized, and charming nursery. My parents were delighted to prepare a place for their newest granddaughter and that is exactly how God feels about each of His children. Jesus tells us that He has gone to make ready a place for us and He promises to come and take us with Him to paradise. What a beautiful reality eternity will be!

"Our Lord has written the promise of the resurrection not in books alone, but in every leaf in the springtime."
-Martin Luther

Prayer

Dear Jesus,

Thank You for preparing a place for me in heaven. I imagine the angels rejoicing at every baptism when a child is welcomed into Your family. Help me to delight in the promise of my salvation as I await the future. Watch over my precious child and keep me steadfast in Your word and in prayer. Amen.

Song

MercyMe. "I Can Only Imagine." *Almost There*. Provident Music Distribution, 2001. CD.

Week 12 Day 1

"Cast your cares on the Lord and he will sustain you; he will never let the righteous fall." (Ps. 55.22)

Are you weary of feeling nauseated and vomiting? Do you find yourself groaning to the Lord, "But I call to God, and the Lord saves me. Evening, morning and noon I cry out in distress, and He hears my voice..." (Ps. 55.16-17)

During my first pregnancy, I often complained about my morning sickness. I remember even confessing to my husband through tear filled eyes, "I can't do this!" He lovingly held me in his arms and simply stated, "You kind of have to now." God was gently preparing me for a more difficult, high-risk pregnancy in the future.

Do not be afraid to bring your fears and concerns to your loving Savior. "...he will sustain you; he will never let the righteous fall." God always gives you the strength you need to complete the tasks He has given you.

Prayer
Merciful Savior,

Hear my prayer! Help me endure this morning sickness. Please give my body and mind rest. Take my worries and fill my heart with Your peace and the assurance of Your presence. Sustain me during this trying experience and give me the faith I need to trust in You. I pray that my baby may know You as his Savior, so that he may spend eternity with You. In Jesus' name, amen.

Song
Carrollton. "Holding On To You." *Sunlight and Shadows.* Centricity Music, 2015. CD.

Week 12 Day 2

"He tends his flock like a shepherd: He gathers the lambs in his arms and carries them close to his heart; he gently leads those that have young." (Isa. 40.11)

What a beautiful description of how your Heavenly Father cares for you! "…he gently leads those that have young…" When you understand how much your Savior loves you, it is much easier to follow where He leads. If you are exhausted or wounded, the Bible says that He carries you "…close to his heart…" Out of His infinite compassion, God willingly bears your burdens and helps you in the midst of every pain. As your Good Shepherd, He stays close to you and guides you to green pastures with peaceful waters.

Prayer
Dear Jesus,
Thank You for leading me with a tender hand and for carrying me when I am too weak to follow on my own. It is comforting to know You hold my child and me close to Your heart. Help us to always remain in Your love. Amen.

Song
Schulz, Mark. "Back In His Arms Again." Special Markets Word. 2015. CD.

Week 12 Day 3

"But if from there you seek the Lord your God you will find him if you look for him with all your heart and with all your soul. When you are in distress and all these things have happened to you, then in later days you will return to the Lord your God and obey him. For the Lord your God is a merciful God; he will not abandon or destroy you or forget the covenant with your forefathers..." (Deut. 4.29-31)

During this new season of your life, God encourages you to "seek the Lord...with all your heart..." Then, you will find the peace and hope you are looking for because God is faithful. He will never leave you, nor forsake you. As you prayerfully continue your journey, you will become aware of God's constant presence. It says in Psalms, "I was young and now I am old, yet I have never seen the righteous forsaken or their children begging bread. They are always generous and lend freely; their children will be blessed." (Ps. 37.25-26)

Later, after your child has been born, you will lead your child to her Savior. Her eternal destiny begins with you sharing your faith. Therefore, teach her to seek the Lord with all her heart and all her soul by your example. Tell your legacy how you prayed for her while she was growing in your womb and share your story of God's faithfulness.

"Setting an example is not the main means of influencing another, it is the only means."
-Albert Einstein

Prayer

Dear Jesus,

Help me to pursue Your wisdom and Your word. Enflame my heart with the desire to pray and the need to commune with You. Lead me to worship You and to follow You all of my days. I want my children to spend eternity with You and me in heaven. Help me to guide them and to teach them Your truths. Amen.

Song

Tree 63. "Blessed Be Your Name." *The Answer to the Question.* InPop Records, 2004. CD.

Week 12 Day 4

"The Lord delights in those who fear him, who put their hope in his unfailing love." (Ps. 147.11)

God is not impressed with self-confidence. Rather, He delights in those who trust in Him because of His "unfailing love." Growing up I was taught that I was to fear, love, and trust God. Initially, I feared His almighty power and omniscience more than I ever loved or trusted Jesus. It wasn't until I recognized His tender display of affection through my blessings that I truly believed God loved me dearly.

Think about your life's journey thus far and search for the evidence of His unfailing love. You will be overwhelmed when you start to see the treasures God has carefully woven into your life. Your baby is yet another confirmation of the Heavenly Father's great love for you.

"A little while with Jesus-Oh, how it soothes the soul and gathers all the threads of life into a perfect whole."
-Lina Sandell

Prayer

Dear Lord Jesus,

Thank You for Your perfect love and faithfulness. You have been so good to me in spite of myself. Thank You for taking care of me. I pray You will bless my unborn child and surround her with Your love and protection. Amen.

Song

Crowder, David. "How He Loves." Passion: Awakening. Six Steps Records, 2010. CD.

Week 12 Day 5

"I wait for the Lord, my soul waits, and in his word I put my hope." (Ps. 130.5)

These next several months may pass very slowly as you wait for such a wonderful blessing, but God uses time to prepare your heart and mind. When I learned there was a good chance I would be confined to bed rest, I readily began preparing the nursery months in advance. I wish I had realized how much more my soul needed to be immersed in the word of God. When I did pursue God's word, I felt encouraged and uplifted. I began to understand that "No one whose hope is in you will ever be put to shame." (Ps. 25.3) As Christians, we can trust in God's faithfulness because our Savior has risen from the dead. Because He is alive all His promises are still true today!

Prayer
Lord,
I am eagerly awaiting this child's arrival day. I pray that her life will be filled with Your love and mercies. Help me to confidently put my hope in You and the promise of a joyful eternity with You in heaven. Let our days in this world be joyful as we look forward to our heavenly home. Watch over the dear child You have given me. In Jesus' name, amen.

Song
Waller, John. "While I'm Waiting." *While I'm Waiting*. Beach Street, 2009. CD.

2nd Trimester

Week 13 Day 1

"For by him all things were created; things in heaven and on earth, visible and invisible, whether thrones or powers or rulers or authorities; all things were created by him and for him. He is before all things, and in him all things hold together." (Col. 1.16-17)

After being greatly dismayed by our initial consultation with a perinatologist, we consulted another specialist. At the end of her evaluation she exclaimed, "Your children look beautiful!" What a relief! Even when a child has a possible problem or a deviation from the normal parameters, mothers need to hear, "Your child is beautiful!"

That is exactly what God is telling you today! He intricately designed your baby and His works are wonderful. God does not make mistakes. He has a plan for your life and your child. "He is before all things, and in him all things hold together."

Prayer

Dear Heavenly Father,

I know Your works are wonderful and I thank You for this child. If there is a problem concerning my baby, I pray You will resolve it according to Your will. I know You can work miracles and that You are holding us in Your arms right now. If it glorifies Your name, please make my baby healthy and strong. Keep my heart steadfast as we walk this road together. In Jesus' name, amen.

Song

Aldous, Rachel. "A Mother's Prayer." *Hannah's Song.* Daywind, CD.

Week 13 Day 2

"Because of your great compassion you did not abandon them in the desert. By day the pillar of cloud did not cease to guide them on their path, nor the pillar of fire by night to shine on the way they were to take. You gave your good Spirit to instruct them. You did not withhold your manna from their mouths, and you gave them water for their thirst. For forty years you sustained them in the desert; they lacked nothing..." (Neh. 9.10-21)

For forty years God supplied provisions and guidance to the Israelites. Perhaps the normal duration of a pregnancy is forty weeks because the number forty signifies completeness in the Bible. If God sustained the Israelites until their desert journey was complete, will He not also graciously sustain you during your pregnancy? God's faithfulness is unchanging and His compassion for you knows no bounds. He loves you fully and unconditionally through the grace of Christ. God has given you the gift of His Holy Spirit and the Bible to guide, strengthen, and fulfill you. Rest in His favor as you continue in your second trimester.

Prayer
Lord,
Thank You for providing for my every need. Please help me to trust in You and to hunger for Your words of truth and reassurance. I love You, Lord Jesus. Amen.

Song
Tree63. "Blessed Be Your Name." *The Answer to the Question.* InPop Records, 2004. CD.

Week 13 Day 3

"So the other disciples told him, "We have seen the Lord!"
But he said to them, "Unless I (Thomas) see the nail marks in
his hands and put my finger where the nails were, and put my
hand into his side, I will not believe it." A week later his
disciples were in the house again, and Thomas was with them.
Though the doors were locked, Jesus came and stood among
them and said, "Peace be with you!" Then he said to Thomas,
"Put your finger here; see my hands. Reach out your hand
and put it into my side. Stop doubting and believe." Thomas
said to him, "My Lord and my God!" Then Jesus told him,
"Because you have seen me, you have believed; blessed are
those who have not seen and yet have believed." Jesus did
many other miraculous signs in the presence of his disciples,
which are not recorded in this book. But these are written that
you may believe that Jesus is the Christ, the Son of God, and
that by believing you may have life in his name."
(John 20.25-31)

By the third month all the internal parts are formed and
continue to develop. The hands are more developed than the
feet and they continue to grow along with the muscles and
nails. (American College of Obstetricians and Gynecologists,
web)

Isn't it fascinating that Thomas asked to touch the
wounds in Jesus' hands when he needed to validate the
resurrection of his Savior? From the very beginning, the
agility of your fingers enables you to confirm what your eyes
see and sometimes what your heart believes. Does your
ability to feel the tiny flutter of your baby's movement make
this pregnancy more of a reality?

Look also in this passage at how Jesus handled Thomas' doubt. He greeted him, "Peace be with you...put your finger in my hands...stop doubting and believe." Jesus addressed Thomas' unbelief with patience and a commanding presence. He wanted Thomas to have peace, just like you.

What would it be like to see Jesus and have the opportunity to ask Him your greatest questions regarding the future? Jesus said blessed is he who believes without seeing. The Bible reassures you of your Savior's presence and your salvation even when you cannot see His face or touch His hands.

Prayer
Dear Jesus,

Please touch my heart with Your loving hand and reassure me of Your presence. Thank You for lovingly forming this miracle inside of me. Help me to follow You, even when doubt plagues me. Keep me steadfast in Your word. Amen.

Song
Schultz, Mark. "Back In His Arms Again." *Studio Series*. Word Records, 2010. CD.

Week 13 Day 4

"A heart at peace gives life to the body, but envy rots the bones." (Prov. 15.13)

Are you jealous of someone? Are you envious of another woman's uncomplicated pregnancy or seemingly effortless ability to have children? It's in our sinful nature to want what we don't have. Society reinforces our selfish desires and convinces us that we deserve to have it all. Eve's life was perfect in the Garden of Eden and yet, she sacrificed everything to gain even more. God wants you to be content with what He has provided for you because He wants you to be happy. Now that sin has entered the world, no life is flawless. "But may the righteous be glad and rejoice before God; may they be happy and joyful." (Ps. 68.3)

I heard it said once that "I am not thankful because I am happy. I am happy because I am thankful." What do you have to be thankful for? When you are feeling the bitter sting of jealousy, repent and seek God's forgiveness. Only then will your heart be able to feel the true joy that comes from being thankful and content.

Prayer

Lord,

Thank you for this baby. Help me always to remember what a blessing this child is in my life. Please forgive me when I am discontent and help me to dwell on the blessings You have given me. In Jesus' name, amen.

Song

Casting Crowns. "Life of Praise." *Casting Crowns.* Beach Street Records, 2003. CD.

Week 13 Day 5

"What other nation is so great as to have their gods near them the way the Lord our God is near us whenever we pray to him?" (Deut. 4.7)

What is your prayer today? Perhaps, if you are like me, you find it difficult to focus on your conversation with God because you are distracted by life's obligations. I urge you to consider keeping a prayer journal, setting aside a specific prayer time, and even praying audibly. God already knows your needs, but He longs for you to open your heart and mind to Him in honest conversations. He has promised to listen because He cares for you and your baby.

"God waits. God listens. God speaks. Relax and enter God's presence." (Karpenko, 9)

Prayer
Dear Lord,
Surround me with your presence. I lift up my life and this child to You. Please protect my baby and keep him safe, and healthy, and strong. In Jesus' name, amen.

Song
Mandisa. "He is With You." *Freedom*. Sparrow, 2009. CD.

Week 14 Day 1

"You prepare a table before me in the presence of my enemies. You anoint my head with oil; my cup overflows. Surely goodness and love will follow me all the days of my life, and I will dwell in the house of the Lord forever." (Ps. 23.5-6)

During your pregnancy you will be offered the triple screen test to check for certain anomalies found in unborn babies. Some mothers will choose to undergo this screening to help alleviate their fears or to give themselves ample time to prepare for a child with special needs. However, if the test results reveal the presence of unfavorable conditions, mothers could also be given the option of terminating the pregnancy. This choice is from our greatest enemy...Satan. In the Garden of Eden it was Satan who tempted Eve with the knowledge of good and evil because human nature desires omniscience and control.

If you choose to undergo these screenings to reassure yourself, remember that no earthly test can give you the peace that passes all understanding. That kind of comfort only comes from trusting in your Savior, Jesus. No test results can ever nullify God's faithfulness. For "Surely goodness and love will follow me all the days of my life, and I will dwell in the house of the Lord forever."

Prayer

Dear Jesus,

Please help me to trust in You. Enable me to rest in the promises You have given. Calm my fears and allow me to believe You love us in every circumstance. Remind me that no matter what the future brings, You are in control. I know You have a beautiful plan for our lives. Help me to follow You everyday. This child is so precious to You and to me. Please watch over him. Amen.

Song

Gokey, Danny. "Hope in Front of Me." *Hope in Front of Me.* BMG Rights Management, 2014. CD.

Week 14 Day 2

"Humble yourselves therefore, under God's mighty hand, that he may lift you up in due time. Cast all your anxiety on him because he cares for you." (1 Pet. 5.6-7)

Before I knew I was pregnant with twins, I had decided I needed to resume working outside of the home. Even though God was telling me He had a different plan, I was determined not to relinquish control over my life. However, at 6 weeks, my ultrasound revealed God's grand design. We were having twins! Suddenly, I was a high-risk pregnancy. Thankfully, God was not dissuaded by my intentions.

My prayer is that you will trust your life to the Lord and anticipate His great blessings. Seek His guidance and then listen to His voice. He cares for you and your child deeply. Let Him carry your burdens as you remain in the palm of His mighty hand.

Prayer

Dear Heavenly Father,

I know Your ways are not my ways and Your thoughts are not my thoughts. Yet, I long to walk with You. Shape my heart's desires to align with Your will so that I may be a woman after Your own heart. Please guard and protect my precious child as we continue on this journey together. In Jesus' name, amen.

Song

TobyMac. "Me Without You." *Eye On It*. Forefront Records, 2012. CD.

Week 14 Day 3

"But as for you, continue in what you have learned and have become convinced of, because you know those from whom you learned it, and how from infancy you have known the Holy Scriptures, which are able to make you wise for salvation through faith in Christ Jesus." (2 Tim. 3.14-15)

In the past when God's design was different than what I planned, I had to rely on what I had been taught about the Christian faith. The support of other Christians in my life has been invaluable. I remember when I was young and struggling with a difficult decision, my father said, "The choice is not right or wrong, but right or left." His wisdom helped me to understand that when you walk in faith, God promises to always be near you. Sometimes, the answer is unclear or uncertain, but we know God is with us. When we feel as though our faith is being challenged, we can have confidence in the gospel because we know the people from whom we've learned the truth. We are not alone. We are part of the Christian church and that is a source of great power and encouragement. Think of the people God has placed in your life to lead you to salvation. How have they lifted you up over the years? How has their example impressed upon you the faithfulness of your Savior? If you need to feel the loving arms of God, reach out to one of your spiritual heroes or your church family. They will present your requests to God in prayer and surround you with the love of Christ Jesus.

Prayer
Dear Lord,

Thank you for the Christian examples You have placed in my life. Make me a light to those around me as we seek to serve you. May I be my child's first Christian hero. In Jesus' name, amen.

Song
NeedtoBreathe. "Brother." *Rivers In the Wasteland.* Atlantic Records, 2014. CD.

Week 14 Day 4

"I pray that out of his glorious riches he may strengthen you with power through his Spirit in your inner being, so that Christ may dwell in your hearts through faith. And I pray that you, being rooted and established in love, may have power, together with all the saints, to grasp how wide and long and high and deep is the love of Christ, and to know this love that surpasses knowledge-that you may be filled to the measure of all the fullness of God." (Eph. 3.16-19)

Love is something we all desire. Christ's love is perpetual and He is faithful, even when we are not. I pray that you will dwell in Christ's love through the Holy Spirit. May your heart be so full of gratitude that joy will overflow from your lips. Even when it is difficult to understand God's ways, abide in His love and proclaim to the world, "For God so loved the world that he gave his one and only Son, that whoever believes in him shall not perish but have eternal life." (John 3.16)

"Children are love made visible."
–American proverb

Prayer
Dear Christ,
    Thank You for loving me unceasingly and for this beautiful blessing growing within me. Please strengthen me with Your Holy Spirit and fill my heart with joy. Amen.

Song
Big Daddy Weave. "Overwhelmed." *Love Come to Life*. Fervent Records, 2012. CD.

Week 14 Day 5

"...Do not think that because you are in the king's house you alone of all the Jews will escape. For if you remain silent at this time, relief and deliverance for the Jews will arise from another place, but you and your father's family will perish. And who knows but that you have come to royal position for such a time as this?" (Esth. 4.12-14)

In the book of Esther, a beautiful young Jew became the chosen Queen of the Persian King Xerxes. During her reign she concealed her ethnicity according to her guardian, Mordecai's wishes. However, when Mordecai discovered a plot against the Jewish people, he persuaded Esther to plead with King Xerxes, for "...who knows but that you have come to royal position for such a time as this?" He recognized the significance Esther's position could have in achieving God's purpose and he testified to the divine influence God had in ensuring the deliverance of the Jews.

God has chosen you specifically to be the mother of this child. "...who knows but that you have come to royal position for such a time as this?" No one else has been given this honor or responsibility. May you celebrate your destiny!

I encourage you to read the book of Esther and learn more about her story. Mordecai's request jeopardized Esther's life, position, marital relationship, and safety. Perhaps this pregnancy feels a little precarious at times too. When you are discouraged, think of Esther. God was able to use her to achieve His purpose because she was willing to trust her Lord in very difficult circumstances. Are you willing to trust God?

Prayer

Dear Jesus,

I know You have placed me in this position for such a time as this. I surrender my life and my will to Your plan. Help me to trust in Your unfailing love. Protect my child and give me the peace that can only come from You. In Jesus' name, amen.

Song

Casting Crowns. "Thrive." *Thrive*. Reunion Records, 2014. CD.

Week 15 Day 1

"How lovely is your dwelling place, O Lord Almighty! My soul yearns, even faints, for the courts of the Lord; my heart and my flesh cry out for the living God. Even the sparrow has found a home, and the swallow a nest for herself, where she may have her young-a place near your altar, O Lord Almighty, my King and my God. Blessed are those who dwell in your house; they are ever praising you. Blessed are those whose strength is in you, who have set their hearts on pilgrimage." (Ps. 84.1-5)

Are you beginning your nesting preparations in anticipation of your precious baby? Pregnancy is an exciting and sometimes overwhelming adventure. As you eagerly build a beautiful home for your child, remember that is important for you to spend time dwelling in the Lord's house as well. If that is not possible, do your best to spend time with Jesus. Let Him fill your heart and mind with His promises and truths for "…unless the Lord builds the house, its builders labor in vain…" (Ps. 127.1)

Prayer
Dear Jesus,
I can only imagine how amazing heaven will be! As I prepare a place for my child on earth, I know you are preparing a place for my child and me. Help me to be ever mindful of my future salvation and to build our home on your word and promises. Amen.

Song
MercyMe. "I Can Only Imagine." *The Worship Project*. 1999. CD.

Week 15 Day 2

"I sought the Lord, and he answered me; he delivered me from all my fears." (Ps. 34.4)

There was a point during my pregnancy when the Lord "...delivered me from all my fears..." Prior to that moment, I actively sought out treatments and solutions to potential complications. Yet the more I planned, the less prepared I felt. Fear and frustration overwhelmed me. Surprisingly, God used Job 39.1-4 to reveal His great love to me. "Do you know when the mountain goats give birth? Do you watch when the doe bears her fawn? Do you count the months till they bear? Do you know the time they give birth? They crouch down and bring forth their young; their labor pains are ended. Their young thrive and grow strong in the wilds; they leave and do not return."

Through this passage, I could see God's great concern for everything He made because He actually counted the months until a deer gave birth. If God knew when an animal would bring forth her baby, surely He was mindful of us. I took great comfort in knowing my Creator was keeping track of the time during my pregnancy, even though He already knew the designated day. He was aware of every movement my children made as well as every pain and concern I experienced. Then, when I read how God continued to watch over the growing fawn, I was finally convinced that God was mindful of my children's well-being too. The Powerful and Merciful Creator cared for us and would continue to be involved in our lives, even after my children were born!

In His great mercy, God lovingly opened my eyes. "The Lord is gracious and compassionate, slow to anger and rich in love. The Lord is good to all; he has compassion on all he has made." (Ps.145.8-9)

God helped me see that He was in control. When I finally relinquished the lives of my children to the care of their Heavenly Father, I found peace. I knew and believed that God would be there in every circumstance. I didn't need to be afraid.

Prayer

Dear Heavenly Father,

Help me to surrender to Your will and to trust in Your faithfulness. I know You are a God of compassion and love. Help me to find strength, reassurance, and courage in Your word and promises. "There is surely a future hope for you and your hope will not be cut off." (Prov. 23.18)

In Jesus' name, amen.

Song

Hillsong. "I Give You My Heart." *Christian Music's Best Worship*. Star Song Music, 2013. Music download.

Week 15 Day 3

"Blessed is he whose help is the God of Jacob, whose hope is in the Lord his God, the Maker of heaven and earth, the seas, and everything in them-the Lord remains faithful forever." (Ps. 146.5-6)

You are blessed, dear woman, because the Creator of heaven and earth cares for you. The Covenant God of Jacob has promised to remain forever faithful. He will never leave you, nor forsake you. God has lovingly and meticulously created this new life within you. Right now your child has fine hair, called lanugo, on his head; his bones are hardening; his liver and pancreas are making secretions; and he is even making sucking motions!
(U.S. National Library of Medicine, Web)

The Omnipotent Creator of the Universe lovingly calls you by your name. He knows you and your child intimately.

Prayer
Dear Creator God,
"When I consider your heavens, the work of your fingers, the moon and the stars, which you have set in place, what is man that you are mindful of him, the son of man that you care for him?" (Ps. 8.3-4) Lord, thank You for remembering me and fashioning this little child of mine. Please watch over him as he grows and help me to trust in Your faithfulness. In Jesus' name, amen.

Song
Battistelli, Francesca. "He Knows My Name." *If We're Honest.* Fervent Records, 2014. CD.

Week 15 Day 4

"Now to him who is able to do immeasurably more than all we ask or imagine according to his power that is at work within us, to him be glory in the church and in Christ Jesus throughout all generations, for ever and ever! Amen." (Eph. 3.20)

When the specialist outlined the percentages of various complications associated with multiple births I was shaken. Fortunately, my husband insisted we find another doctor. As a devout man of God, he felt that our medical advisors should not address possible problems until they were evident. However, I immediately proceeded to research all of the potential complications and devise possible solutions. I was so concerned with impending difficulties that I could not celebrate the pregnancy. Then God provided a Christian perinatologist to continue our care. Thankfully, God helped me remember all the things He had done. The God who placed the stars in motion and made the land and seas was completely capable of making two perfect babies inside of me. The relief I felt when I finally believed God was in control was indescribable. I knew God was sovereign and the outcome of this pregnancy was part of His glorious design. He could make them healthy and strong if that was His will. Or, He would give us the strength and ability needed to raise children with special needs. Ultimately, I knew I had to submit to His plan and rest in His loving embrace. Now you must trust God also. Remember that God is omniscient and He knows what is happening inside your womb, even when the specialists are uncertain. Throughout your pregnancy your Savior is holding you in His tender care as your precious baby grows.

Prayer

Dear Heavenly Father,

I know You are a powerful and loving God. I pray that if it is Your will, You will help my baby grow healthy and strong. Let me carry this baby to term and grant me the strength only You can provide. Thank You for hearing my prayer and help me to rest securely in Your loving and merciful embrace. In Jesus' name, amen.

Song

Mandisa. "He Is With You." *Freedom.* Sparrow, 2009. CD.

Week 15 Day 5

"Do not be afraid or terrified because of them, for the Lord your God goes with you; he will never leave you nor forsake you...do not be discouraged." (Deut. 31.6-8)

Many obstetric offices encourage patients to schedule their prenatal appointments with various healthcare providers employed within their office. This method of care helps familiarize patients with several of the professionals who could potentially deliver a child. I quickly became frustrated with this process when I was repeatedly greeted with the same question, "So you're having twins?" This left me feeling uneasy and vulnerable. Consequently, I had to acknowledge who my real provider was. The truth is, no matter who is responsible for the delivery of your child, God is still in control. He doesn't need a chart to remember your health history or to monitor your progress. He is fully aware and involved in the well-being of you and your child.

It is beneficial to pray for the competence and ability of the staff taking providing your care. Ask God to bless the work of their hands and give them the wisdom they need. God has promised to "...never leave you nor forsake you..." so embrace this journey with courage because you are not alone.

Prayer

Dear Jesus,

You have promised to walk me through this pregnancy. I ask You to give me courage to face this challenge. Bless the medical team with sound minds and compassionate spirits. Help them to bring my child into this world to the best of their abilities. Give me peace and guard my heart with the promise of Your faithfulness. Amen.

Song

Norman, Bebo. "I Will Lift My Eyes." *Between the Dreaming and Coming True*. Essential Records, 2006. CD.

Week 16 Day 1

"Father, if you are willing, take this cup from me; yet not my will, but yours be done." (Luke 22.42)

On the night Jesus was betrayed and handed over to His enemies, this was His prayer. In the Garden of Gethsemane Jesus pleaded with His Heavenly Father to save Him from the immense suffering and sorrow He knew was coming. Jesus longed for God to turn His face towards Him and be merciful. Yet in spite of His fear, Jesus chose to submit to God's will and die in your place and mine. What greater love could there be?

Are you frightened by the term "high-risk" like I was? Does your heart despair with the statistics and probabilities professionals present? Take courage, for God says in His word, "So do not fear, for I am with you; do not be dismayed, for I am your God. I will strengthen you and help you; I will uphold you with my righteous right hand." (Isa. 41.10) God promises to never leave you nor forsake you. He will give you strength just as He did with His own Son, Jesus. For it says in Luke, "An angel from heaven appeared to him and strengthened him." (Luke 22.43) In His greatest need, God did not abandon His Son and He will not abandon you. God has a special purpose for your life and He will walk with you on this journey.

Prayer
Lord Jesus,

Walk with me. Please be my shield. Protect me from the arrows of despair and fear. Help me to be strong in the faith and give me the courage I need to surrender this child to Your will. For I know You love my baby more than I do because You died to save my child. Please help me to remember Your great mercies and cover me in Your peace. Amen.

Song
David Crowder Band. "How He Loves." *Passion: Awakening.* Six Steps Records, 2010. Cd.

Week 16 Day 2

"Your ways, O God, are holy. What god is so great as our God? You are the God who performs miracles; you display your power among the peoples. With your mighty arm you redeemed your people...Your path led through the sea, your way through the mighty waters, though your footprints were not seen. You led your people like a flock by the hand of Moses and Aaron." (Ps. 77.13-20)

Do you remember the story of Moses leading the Israelites out of captivity in Egypt to the promise land? God did not choose a simple path for His people. He held back the mighty waters of the Red Sea to bring His people out of bondage. Although they did not see God, they knew He was guiding them.

God may not have chosen the easiest path for you, but look for His footprints. Even if it seems as if waves are crashing down around you, God is with you. Follow where He leads while trusting in His perfect love and power.

Prayer

God,

I have heard the stories of Your mighty deeds and I believe in You. I know You can carry me through this and I pray You will guide my footsteps. Please protect my child and help me to submit to Your ways because I know You care for me. Hold back the waves and lead us down Your path, dear Jesus. Amen.

Song

Love & the Outcome. "He Is With Us." *Love & the Outcome.* Word Records, 2013. CD.

Week 16 Day 3

"Trust in the Lord with all your heart and lean not on your own understanding; in all your ways acknowledge him, and he will make your paths straight." (Prov. 3.5-6)

Our society encourages people to be self-reliant and ambitious. When you are faced with difficulties do you feel obligated to solve your own problems? If you fail to acknowledge your complete dependency on a merciful Savior, you are limited by your human capabilities. God is able to resolve every difficult circumstance, but sometimes He allows you to struggle in an effort to draw you closer to Him. Only when you acknowledge God as the source of all your blessings and commit your life to serving Him, are you able to confidently walk with the Lord down straight paths.

Prayer

Dear Jesus,

Thank You for dying on the cross for my sins. Thank You for being my Savior. Help me to follow You all of the days of my life. Please watch over my child and me as we continue with You on this journey. Amen.

Song

Battistelli, Fancesca. "Strangely Dim." *Hundred More Years*. Word Entertainment, 2011. CD.

Week 16 Day 4

"But Jesus immediately said to them: "Take courage! It is I. Don't be afraid." "Lord, if it's you," Peter replied, "tell me to come to you on the water." "Come," he said." (Matt. 14.27-29)

When you found out you were pregnant, did you feel like Peter when he saw Jesus walking on water? Were you excited and eager to accept God's invitation to motherhood? Then, after your first visit with the perinatologist, did your enthusiasm start to waver because the future was uncertain? You are not alone. It says, "Then Peter got down out of the boat, walked on the water and came toward Jesus. But when he saw the wind, he was afraid and, beginning to sink, cried out, "Lord, save me!" (Matt. 14.29-30)

Since the beginning of time, people have cried out to God to rescue them from their sin, their fears, and their pain. In His infinite mercy, God sent His only Son to die on the cross for your salvation. Jesus did not abandon Peter to drown in his fears. Rather, it says, "...immediately Jesus reached out his hand and caught him..." (Matt. 14.31) God promises to never leave you. Not even for one moment! Peter called out to Jesus, and Jesus responded in love. God's deep concern for you is evident in this remarkable story. Only after Jesus rescued Peter, did He say, "You of little faith," he said, "why did you doubt?" And when they climbed into the boat, the wind died down. Then those who were in the boat worshiped him, saying, "Truly you are the son of God." (Matt. 14.31-34)

After surviving some of life's challenges you can testify to God's faithfulness. Contemplate past experiences in which God has saved you in spite of your inadequate faith. Then praise Him! Give Him the glory He deserves and trust your future to Him. Do not let the adversities of this pregnancy keep you from focusing on God. You are safe in His hands.

Prayer
Dear Jesus,

Thank You for rescuing me from my sins and my doubts. Please give me the faith I need to walk on water with You. Don't let the waves of life crash over me. Guard this precious little one that I place in Your hands. Amen.

Song
Camp, Jeremy. "Walk By Faith." *Stay*. BEC Recordings, 2002. CD.

Week 16 Day 5

"He has made everything beautiful in its time. He has also set eternity in the hearts of men; yet they cannot fathom what God has done from beginning to end. I know that there is nothing better for men than to be happy and do good while they live. That everyone may eat and drink, and find satisfaction in all his toil-this is the gift of God."
(Eccles. 3.11-13)

Sometimes when we are consumed by our present hardships, we fail to see the beauty of God's eternal plan. Our human minds are incapable of understanding God's ways because our lives are only a breath. That is why God wants you to enjoy your time on earth. Finding joy in the moment and sharing Christ's love can provide you with immense satisfaction in your everyday life.

Do you wonder why you are experiencing this high-risk pregnancy? Although the biological reasons can often be explained in scientific terms, the spiritual implications might take years to understand. Initially, I wondered why God had chosen to give us twins. I never asked for multiples, and I always appreciated the immense energy and dedication it takes to care for twins. So why did I need to experience a high-risk pregnancy? "And we know that in all things God works for the good of those who love him, who have been called according to his purpose." (Rom. 8.28) Regardless of my limited understanding, "He has made everything beautiful in its time..." I am continually amazed by the joy and fullness that has resulted from raising two sons simultaneously. It is beautiful, and I am so thankful God was not encumbered by my plans and expectations!

Prayer
Dear Jesus,

I don't understand Your celestial design from the beginning of time until now. Just the uncertainties of this pregnancy weigh me down. Please take my anxiety and all my fears as I lay them at Your feet. Your plan is beyond my temporal perspective. Give me eyes to see Your will and a heart to trust You when I am blinded by the present. Amen.

Song
TobyMac. "Beyond Me." *This Is Not a Test*. Forefront Records, 2015. CD.

Week 17 Day 1

"She watches over the affairs of her household and does not eat the bread of idleness." (Prov. 31.27)

Perhaps you are confined to bed rest and you believe that your limited physical activity means you are being idle? Please remember you are doing the one task that no one else on earth can do. Throughout these tedious hours you are nurturing, protecting, loving and providing the perfect environment for your unborn child. This is an overwhelming and worthwhile task that is essential to your baby's well-being. May God give you strength and perseverance.

Hast thou sounded the depths of yonder sea,
And counted the sands that under is be?
Hast thou measured the heights of heaven above?
Then may'st thou mete out a mother's love.
-Emily Taylor

Prayer
Dear God,

This time of inactivity and waiting is passing slowly. I feel idle and bored. Please help me to delight in my calling as the mother and provider of this precious baby. I know the effort I am making is a gift of love. Give me the patience and joy I need to stay committed to this most noble service. In Jesus' name, amen.

Song
West, Matthew. "The Motions." *Something to Say*. Sparrow Records, 2008. CD.

Week 17 Day 2

"Why are you downcast, O my soul? Why so disturbed within me? Put your hope in God, for I will yet praise him, my Savior & my God." (Ps. 42.5)

There are times in life when it is difficult to verbalize your emotions. Sometimes you cannot even explain the source of your anguish. In those moments, it is good to remember that when "...we do not know what we ought to pray for, but the Spirit himself intercedes for us with groans that words cannot express. And he who searches our hearts knows the mind of the Spirit, because the Spirit intercedes for the saints in accordance with God's will." (Rom. 8.26-27)

In the words above you can see how tirelessly God seeks to comfort you. The Holy Spirit intercedes on your behalf to help you communicate your deepest feelings. Your Heavenly Father hears your prayers and understands your needs, even when others fail to comprehend your struggle. Praise the God who sees inside of you and redeems you. May His sincere regard for your well-being uplift your soul and strengthen your faith.

Prayer

Dearest Savior,

Thank You for investing so much energy in me and patiently listening to my prayers. Lord, You know my heart. Please forgive me for my sins and renew a right spirit within me. May my life be a celebration of all You have done for me as a redeemed child of God. Free me from my worries and strengthen me in my weakness. Watch over this precious child of mine and grant him a full and blessed life, according to Your will. Amen.

Song

Story, Laura. "Blessings." *Blessings*. Fair Trade Services, 2011. CD.

Week 17 Day 3

"Do you not know? Have you not heard? The Lord is the everlasting God, the Creator of the ends of the earth. He will not grow tired or weary, and his understanding no one can fathom. He gives strength to the weary and increases the power of the weak. Even youths grow tired and weary, and young men stumble and fall; but those who hope in the Lord will renew their strength. They will soar on wings like eagles; they will run and not grow weary, they will walk and not be faint." (Isa. 40.28-31)

Are you completely exhausted and yet still you find it difficult to rest comfortably? Take heart! The Lord will renew your strength for His power never fails. Can you imagine never feeling weak or tired? What a comfort it is to know that God can readily sustain you. Prayerfully beseech Him to endow you with vigor so that you may "...press on toward the goal to win the prize for which God has called me heavenward in Christ Jesus." (Phil. 3.14) God is faithful and He will provide the energy you need.

Prayer

Almighty God,
I am weary and my journey is not complete. Please sustain me in this pregnancy. Give me the strength I need to do the tasks You have called me to do and to grow this child. Help me to always draw my strength from You. May Your gracious love surround us. In Jesus' name, amen.

Song

Philips, Craig, and Dean. "You are God Alone." *Let the Worshippers Arise*. Fair Trade Services, 2004. CD.

Week 17 Day 4

"His master replied, `Well done, good and faithful servant! You have been faithful with a few things, I will put you in charge of many things. Come and share your master's happiness…'" (Matt. 25.21)

My sister was on bed rest for several months of her high-risk pregnancy. She told me of a time when she complained to a fellow mother about her boredom, frustration and anxiety. The woman had also endured similar circumstances and replied curtly, "If you are not ready to be on bed rest, then you are not ready to be a mom."

I was taken aback by the harsh words spoken to my gentle sibling, but there is something to be gleaned from her statement. The outcome and factors within a pregnancy are often outside your control, but there are times when your commitment to bed rest, good nutrition, and following a doctor's orders can dramatically influence the health of your child.

Thankfully, my sister was rewarded for her diligent inactivity and commitment to a grueling medicinal regimen upon the birth of her children. She treasures them greatly and does not begrudge the time she invested during her pregnancy. Now, God has put her "…in charge of many things…" as she delights in raising the sons God has given her. God has a plan. Be strong and courageous for God is with you!

Prayer

Dear Jesus,

I am tired and worn out. This pregnancy is difficult and requires more than I feel I can give. But I know that You restore the strength and spirit of those who seek You. Lord, help me! Keep me committed to growing this baby so that I may have the opportunity to raise my precious child of God. Give me a spirit of joy and determination. Help my mind and days be filled with things that bring You glory and give me peace. Amen.

Song

Sidewalk Prophets. "Help Me Find It." *Live Like That.* Word Entertainment. 2012. CD.

Week 17 Day 5

"I rejoice in your promise like one who finds great spoil."
(Ps. 119.162)

In recent years I have heard it said, "Trust in the promises of God." Somewhat perplexed, I found myself asking, "What are the promises of God?" As I searched the scriptures and listened intently to sermons, I realized that God promises to wash away all our sins and cleanse us from our unrighteousness. If we believe in Jesus Christ as our Lord and Savior we will spend eternity in heaven with Him. He also pledges, "I will never leave you, nor forsake you." (Jos. 1.5) That promise will see you through every circumstance and every challenge. He does not guarantee a life free from sorrow, but He is committed to traveling with you until you reach the promised land. You know the destination, but only God knows the path you will take. When you trust in His faithfulness and the great love He has for you, then you will see the beauty of the journey. Rejoice because your Savior is walking with you. That is His promise!

Prayer
Lord,
Thank You for being my Shepherd and my Guide. Help me to trust in Your promises and to rejoice in Your loving guidance. Please walk with me as we continue on this pregnancy journey. Show me the beauty along the way and help me to recognize Your presence. In Jesus' name, amen.

Song
Stanfill, Kristian. "One Thing Remains." *Passion: White Flag*. Six Step Records, 2012. CD.

Week 18 Day 1

"I praise you because I am fearfully and wonderfully made; your works are wonderful, I know that full well. My frame was not hidden from you when I was made in the secret place. When I was woven together in the depths of the earth, your eyes saw my unformed body. All the days ordained for me were written in your book before one of them came to be. How precious to me are your thoughts, O god! How vast is the sum of them!" (Ps. 139.14-17)

Perhaps you have recently had a sonogram to evaluate your child's development. Although it is often referred to as an anatomy scan, it is much more significant to an expectant mother. It is a breath-taking glimpse of your precious baby moving and growing within you.

Consider the images you saw on the screen and know that God sees your child even more clearly because He fashioned your child with His own hands. He lovingly created your baby with His purpose in mind. No matter what the sonogram displays, it cannot negate how intentionally and compassionately God formed your child. God has a plan for each of His children. We are all here to bring glory to God.

"The child must know that he is a miracle, that since the beginning of the world there hasn't been, and until the end of the world there will not be, another child like him."
-Pablo Casals

Prayer

Dear Creator God,

Thank You for lovingly shaping my child. I cannot wait to meet him! You have made my baby in Your own image, and I know You have a special plan for him. Please help me to cherish the unique qualities You have placed in my child and protect him as he continues to grow in the secret place. Forgive me for the times when I do not acknowledge You as the Divine Creator. In Jesus' name, amen.

Song

Redman, Matt. "Fearfully and Wonderfully Made." *Beautiful News*. Six Step Records, 2006. CD.

Week 18 Day 2

"God is our refuge and strength, an ever-present help in trouble. Therefore we will not fear, though the earth give way and the mountains fall into the heart of the sea, though its waters roar and foam and the mountains quake with their surging." (Ps. 46.1-2)

This passage is a powerful and vivid confession of a fearless trust in God. I am deeply humbled by the constant presence of my Savior through difficult and painful experiences. Through these moments I have become keenly aware of God's genuine concern for my welfare.

Reflect on a time when you felt helpless and God delivered you. Take comfort in that memory, for God loves you and your baby dearly. He will continue to be your refuge and strength as you continue on your pregnancy journey.

"We delight in the beauty of the butterfly, but rarely admit the changes it has gone through to achieve that beauty."
-Maya Angelou

Prayer
Dearest Savior,

Thank You for carrying me through difficult trials and promising to be with me to the end. Help me to recognize Your loving hand creating something wonderful with my life. In Jesus' name, amen.

Song
For King & Country. "Shoulders." *Run Wild. Live Free. Love Strong*. Fervent Records, 2014. CD.

Week 18 Day 3

"...because God has said, "Never will I leave you; never will I forsake you." So we say with confidence, "The Lord is my helper; I will not be afraid. What can man do to me?""
(Heb. 13.5-6)

By now you can probably feel your baby flexing her arms and legs. You might know the gender of your child, and you may have even seen her swallow during a sonogram. I hope your excitement is growing as your belly expands and more maternity clothes begin to fit.

Depending on your circumstance, your enthusiasm might be somewhat diminished. If it is, I implore you to meditate on this verse. When your anxiety overcomes you, rehearse these words in your head or out loud because your child can hear now. God is with you and He will never leave you, nor forsake you. So it's time to celebrate the moment!

Prayer
Dear Lord,

Thank You for the child growing inside of me and the wonder of carrying this baby. Please protect my baby from harm and keep my faith strong. In Jesus' name I pray, amen.

Song
Lincoln Brewster. "Everlasting God." *Let the Praises Ring*. Integrity Music, 2006. CD.

Week 18 Day 4

"Let us fix our eyes on Jesus, the author and perfecter of our faith, who for the joy set before him endured the cross, scorning its shame, and sat down at the right hand of the throne of God. Consider him who endured such opposition from sinful men, so that you will not grow weary and lose heart." (Heb. 12.2-3)

Think of the suffering Jesus willingly endured to ensure your salvation. Christ's humble sacrifice is an encouragement during life's present trials. He will help you to "...not grow weary and lose heart." You must focus on Jesus so that you can persevere in hope. Jesus has overcome death and the grave. Through His sacrifice, you have inherited the kingdom of God. He is greater than all your fears and troubles because He is Lord of all creation. He knew He would suffer, but he consented to the anguish and opposition of sinners to save you. Never doubt how much Jesus loves you or your child!

Prayer
Dear Jesus,
You are my Savior! Thank You for enduring the pain and humiliation of the cross in my place. Please help me to face this challenge with the courage and strength only You can give. Amen.

Song
MercyMe. "Bring the Rain." *Coming Up to Breathe*. Fair Trade Services, 2006. CD.

Week 18 Day 5
Jesus Calms the Storm

"Then he got into the boat and his disciples followed him. Without warning, a furious storm came up on the lake, so that the waves swept over the boat. But Jesus was sleeping. The disciples went and woke him, saying, "Lord, save us! We're going to drown!" He replied, "You of little faith, why are you so afraid?" Then he got up and rebuked the winds and the waves, and it was completely calm. The men were amazed and asked, "What kind of man is this? Even the winds and the waves obey him!" (Matt. 8.23-27)

When you found out you were pregnant were you so overjoyed that you couldn't wait to share the news of your newest blessing? Did your enthusiasm wane when you were suddenly, and possibly unexpectedly, placed in a "high-risk" category? Maybe you felt as I did, swept away in a furious storm of uncertainty? Was your initial response to call out, "Lord, save us!"

Notice what Jesus did in this story. He asked the disciples "...why are you so afraid?" It might seem like a ridiculous question in the midst of a raging storm, but why did Jesus respond in that way? Was He frustrated with the men's lack of faith after witnessing numerous miracles, or was it because He was present in the boat? Jesus is with you in the middle of every crisis. Sometimes God calms our storms, and occasionally He simply remains with us through the waves. God is bigger than your circumstances, and He has promised to be with you in this journey.

My husband's uncle once shared a comical story concerning his wife's prayer for God to go before them and after them on a long road trip. When she had finished praying he asked, "Don't you want him in the car, too?"

Prayer
Lord Jesus,

Save me from my fears and apprehensions. Stay with us on this journey. Calm the storms inside of me with Your peace. The heavenly peace that passes all understanding. If it is Your will, remove these difficult circumstances. If it is not, give me the faith to cling to You as we endure these days together. Lift up my eyes so I may see Your face. Amen.

Song
Casting Crowns. "Praise You in This Storm." *Lifesong*. Reunion Records, 2005. CD.

Week 19 Day 1

"But now, this is what the Lord says-he who created you, O Jacob, he who formed you, O Israel: "Fear not, for I have redeemed you; I have summoned you by name; you are mine. When you pass through the waters, I will be with you; and when you pass through the rivers, they will not sweep over you. When you walk through the fire, you will not be burned; the flames will not set you ablaze. For I am the Lord, your God, the Holy One of Israel, your Savior; I give Egypt for your ransom, Cush and Seba in your stead. Since you are precious and honored in my sight, and because I love you, I will give men in exchange for you, and people in exchange for your life. Do not be afraid, for I am with you..." (Isa. 43.1-5)

What a comforting passage! The Lord not only claims you as His own precious child, but He promises you His faithfulness. There is no circumstance that you will have to face alone. He is always with you because He loves you. When your Creator calls your name and promises to walk with you on life's journey, you have a sense of security and confidence. If you want to be reassured, try saying the passage out loud, while inserting your name.

But now, this is what the Lord says-he who created you, _____, he who formed you, -_____: "Fear not, for I have redeemed you, _____, I have summoned you by name; _____ you are mine. When you pass through the waters, _____ I will be with you; and when you pass through the rivers, _____ they will not sweep over you. When you walk through the fire, _____you will not be burned; the flames will not set you ablaze. For I am the Lord, your God, the Holy One of Israel, your Savior, _____;

I give Egypt for your ransom, Cush and Seba in your stead. Since you are precious and honored in my sight, and because I love you, _____ I will give men in exchange for you, and people in exchange for your life. Do not be afraid, for I am with you, _____.

Prayer
Dear Lord Jesus,

Thank You for promising to walk with me in every situation. May I always trust in Your faithfulness. Sometimes I feel so overwhelmed with my situation and the well-being of my child. Forgive me when I fail to tread boldly along life's path and give me the courage to follow Your lead.
In Jesus' name, amen.

Song
Francesca Battistelli. "Giants Fall." *If We're Honest*. Fervent Records, 2014. CD.

Week 19 Day 2

"Finally, brothers, whatever is true, whatever is noble, whatever is right, whatever is pure, whatever is lovely, whatever is admirable-if anything is excellent or praiseworthy-think about such things." (Phil. 4.8)

God creates women with the ability to discern other people's emotions and needs. This sensitivity allows us to care for children, spouses, and family in our lives. This awareness can also cause us to perseverate on conversations and situations more than necessary. We can easily allow our imperfect relationships with others to consume us. That is why God calls us to purposefully focus our minds on good things. He wants our hearts and minds to be filled with His peace and not burdened with troubles. What will you focus on today? Is there a scripture verse you love? Have you chosen a name for your child?

Prayer

Dear Jesus,

Take over my mind today. Fill it with whatever is noble, true, and good. Free me from my worldly preoccupations and let me celebrate this new life You have created in me. Thank You for my life and the blessings You have graciously bestowed upon me. Amen.

Song

Third Day. "You Are So Good to Me." *Offerings II: All I Have to Give*. Essential Records, 2003. CD.

Week 19 Day 3

"How great is the love that the Father has lavished on us, that we should be called children of God..." (1 John 3.1)

Through the saving grace of Christ, you have been welcomed into the family of God. This is a gift that cannot be earned or taken. In baptism God washes away your sin and fills you with the Holy Spirit. The Holy Spirit creates a living faith in your heart that opens the doors of heaven. God claims you as His child. You are a princess of the King! God wants to share the glory of heaven with you and your child. Therefore, rejoice with your family and your inheritance in the kingdom of God.

Prayer
Dear Heavenly Father,
Thank You for welcoming me into the family of believers through Your saving grace. I am overwhelmed by the love you lavish upon me, and I pray You would cover my child with Your protection and affection. In Jesus' name, amen.

Song
Rend Collective. "Build Your Kingdom Here." *Homemade Worship By Handmade People.* Integrity Music, 2012. CD.

Week 19 Day 4

"...Do not be fainthearted or afraid; do not be terrified or give way to panic before them. For the Lord your God is the one who goes with you to fight for you against your enemies to give you victory." (Deut. 20.3-4)

Sometimes during conversations with certain doctors and family, I felt as though I was defending myself. I would hesitate to call any of them my adversary, but we were definitely not in agreement. There is a time to comply with medical advice, and there is a time to prayerfully evaluate your circumstances. If you are being bombarded with statistics and probabilities, remember that God put the stars that we can't even count, in perfect motion. God has a plan for you and for this baby. God uses doctors and family members to accomplish many wonderful things, but ultimately He is in control. You are not a statistic to God. He is holding your child and you in the palm of His hand. So "...do not be fainthearted or afraid..."

"Statistics are human beings with the tears wiped off."
-Paul Brodeur

Prayer
Dear Jesus,
The statistics and possible complications are so frightening. Please help me to trust in Your sovereignty, while working together with the doctors to keep my baby healthy and strong. Please grant them wisdom and skill. Amen.

Song
Kutless. "Strong Tower." *Strong Tower*. BEC Records, 2005. CD.

Week 19 Day 5

"Peace I leave with you; my peace I give you. I do not give to you as the world gives. Do not let your hearts be troubled and do not be afraid." (John 14.27)

The world yearns for peace. We want peace among the nations, peace in our homes, and peace with others. True contentment, however, is a gift of God through salvation in Christ Jesus. It is difficult to surrender your fears unless you are certain He cares for you and will never forsake you. When you are in fellowship with God, you know your future is in His hands; therefore you can rest safely in His grasp. Only with that assurance can you face the future with confidence and hope.

Prayer

Jesus,

Please give me the gift of Your peace. Help me to rest completely in Your promises and to feel Your presence in my life. Forgive me when I doubt Your goodness and Your mercy. Restore a right spirit within me. Amen.

Song

Passion Worship. "Remember." *Passion: Salvation's Tide is Rising*. Sparrow Records, 2016. CD.

Week 20 Day 1

"So we fix our eyes not on what is seen, but on what is unseen. For what is seen is temporary, but what is unseen is eternal." (2 Cor. 4.18)

Sonograms are a treasured glimpse of what you cannot see. You can feel your beloved baby moving inside you and with each sonogram image your anticipation grows. Sometimes what the doctors see is unsettling. That is when it is most important to fix your eyes on what is unseen. The struggles and pain of this world are real and visible, but so is the merciful love of your Heavenly Father. He loved you enough to sacrifice His Son for you. Jesus paid the ultimate price for your sins and mine. Now, you can spend eternity with Him in heaven. So until that wonderful day comes, focus your mind heavenward and on the promises He has given you. Do not be so transfixed by your limited view of the present that you fail to see God's loving hand reaching out to you in the middle of this journey.

Prayer

Dear Jesus,

Thank You for Your sacrificial love. I am touched by the images of my child. I long to hold my baby in my arms and gaze upon the face You created. Help me to look to You when all I can see is difficulties. Let me seek You always, especially when my heart is burdened. Give me the peace and comfort only You can provide. Amen.

Song

Heath, Brandon. "Give Me Your Eyes." *What If We*. Reunion Records, 2008. CD.

Week 20 Day 2

"Many are the plans in a man's heart, but it is the Lord's purpose that prevails." (Prov. 19.21)

In a book entitled, *The Power of a Positive Mom*, I read one mother's powerful story describing her experience as a mother of a child with special needs. She compared her situation to that of someone who had spent her entire life preparing for a trip to Italy. Consequently, when her plane landed in Holland, rather than Italy, she was utterly disappointed. Holland was not a terrible or unbearable place, but it was not the dream she had anticipated. Yet, when she looked around she discovered that Holland had tulips and Holland had windmills. If she had continued to mourn her lost destiny, she would have never been able to enjoy the beauty of this new place.

Her analogy made a profound impression on me because it reaffirmed what I hope you will always believe. God loves you and your child! He longs to be gracious to you. When life's struggles seem too much to endure, remember to look for the tulips and the windmills.

Prayer
Dearest Lord,

Make Your ways my own. Let me walk in the confidence of a redeemed child of God who is certain of her Father's love and grand design. Bless this little child of mine and bless the one who carries him. In Jesus' name, amen.

Song
Chapman, Steven C. "Something Beautiful." *The Glorious Unfolding*. Reunion Records, 2013. CD.

Week 20 Day 3

"As he went along, he saw a man blind from birth. His disciples asked him, "Rabbi, who sinned, this man or his parents, that he was born blind?" Neither this man nor his parents sinned," said Jesus, "but this happened so that the work of God might be displayed in his life...so the man went and washed, and came home seeing." (John 9.1-7)

Mothers have an innate desire to nurture, comfort, and protect their children. As a result, when their children are hurting, endangered, or disobedient, mothers are inclined to take responsibility. Although we are called to be a loving beacon and a guide in our child's life, we cannot protect them from every painful experience or consequence.

This passage affirms Jesus' great plan for each of His children. Jesus does not punish us for past sins by inflicting disabilities or ailments on our children. We live in an imperfect world. God can even use our imperfections to carry out His purpose. The work of God will be displayed in your life and your child's. I encourage you to ponder the love and compassion that has already been extended to you by fellow Christians during this phase of your life. God uses other people to bless our lives with encouragement and love during times of uncertainty. God is good and perfect and so is His love for you both.

Prayer

Dear Jesus,

I don't understand why we have to suffer. I long for a perfect world, but I know that cannot be until You return in glory. Help me to see Your grace in this sinful world that is sometimes full of pain. Forgive me for my sins and give me the wisdom to trust in Your will for my life. I know my precious baby has a role to play in Your grand design. Help me be a loving presence in his life. Give me the strength I need to be the mom you've called me to be. Be present with our family as we prepare for the coming of this child. Draw us closer together so that we may build a forgiving, caring, and compassionate home. Amen.

Song

Crowder, David. "Come As You Are." *Passion: Take It All*. Six Step Records, 2014. CD.

Week 20 Day 4

"...for man's anger does not bring about the righteous life that God desires." (Jas. 1.20)

"It's not fair! Why can't I have this? What I'm asking for is good. I've done everything I was supposed to! I haven't committed these sins..." Those are the words I screamed at God. I thought I was entitled to the life I wanted because I had lived according to His will. I didn't realize that if I truly received what I deserved I would be dead. For the punishment of sin is death. Yet, in God's great mercy, He graciously provided His Son as atonement for my sins that "...whoever believes in him shall not perish but have eternal life." (John 3.16) God's will for my life was not what I had planned. It was better than I imagined or unfortunately, demanded. Thankfully, over time, God graciously and mercifully transformed my heart.

Are you angry because the Creator has not fashioned your unborn child the way you had hoped? It is our human nature to want to control every aspect of our lives, especially when it pertains to our children. In 1st Peter it is written "Therefore, prepare your minds for action; be self-controlled; set your hope fully on the grace to be given you when Jesus Christ is revealed." (1.13) It is time to prepare for a future in which God's grace will be revealed in a new way. I beseech you to turn to God and not away in the midst of a crisis. God loves you, and He will graciously provide for you and your child.

Prayer

Heavenly Father,

    I do not understand the works of Your hand or Your almighty plan. Do not let my heart be consumed by anger or disappointment. Help me to trust in You and to have hope for the future because I know You care for us.

In Jesus' name, amen.

Song

Downhere. "How Many Kings." *Ending Is Beginning*. Centricity Music, 2008. CD.

Week 20 Day 5

"For everything God created is good, and nothing is to be rejected if it is received with thanksgiving because it is consecrated by the word of God and prayer." (1 Tim. 4.14)

Remember the account of the creation of the world? At the end of every day God said, "It is good." He continues to make all things to benefit His purpose. Sometimes, the sin in this world destroys God's beautiful handiwork. Yet God claims us as His own dear children. "For we are God's workmanship, created in Christ Jesus to do good works, which God prepared in advance for us to do." (Eph. 2.10)

Prayer
Dearest Heavenly Father,
Thank You for fashioning this child with Your loving hands. Help her to grow healthy and strong. Let her life be a light to the world that reflects Your mercy and Your grace. Strengthen her as we await her arrival. In Jesus' name, amen.

Song
Gungor. "Beautiful Things." *Beautiful Things*. Brash Music, 2010. CD.

Week 21 Day 1

"But we have this treasure in jars of clay to show that this all surpassing power is from God and not from us. We are hard pressed on every side, but not crushed, perplexed, but not in despair; persecuted, but not abandoned; struck down, but not destroyed." (2 Cor. 4.7-9)

People often say that God will not give you more than you can bear. Unfortunately, this statement is incredibly misleading because God will give you more than you can bear, but he will not give you more than *He* can bear. God can handle every earthly problem because He has overcome death and the grave. God allows us to face challenges, while offering his help. Let this experience draw you closer to your Savior. For when you recognize your complete dependence on God, He reveals His grace. He mercifully renews you "...though outwardly we are wasting away, yet inwardly we are being renewed day by day..." (2 Cor. 4.16) Every single day, God promises to lovingly restore and strengthen you. He will not leave you to face any trial alone. He suffers alongside of you and gives you the ability to continue down the road of life until the day He calls you home. So walk on faithfully, while you carry the child He has given you.

Prayer

Dear Jesus,

Thank You for being near me in every moment of my life. Help me to lean on You and to trust in Your faithfulness as we continue this journey together. Reach down and touch this life within in me. If it be your will, make her healthy and strong. Create in her a heart that is steadfast and will follow You all the days of her life. Amen.

Song

West, Matthew. "Strong Enough." *The Story of Your Life.* Sparrow Records, 2010. CD.

Week 21 Day 2

"Know that the Lord is God. It is he who made us and we are his; we are his people, the sheep of his pasture." (Ps.100.3)

The same God who spoke the universe into existence has created you and your unborn child. As you stand in awe at the work of His hands, praise Him for the beauty all around you. Your amazing God has purposefully designed a magnificent world, and He has blessed you with senses to enjoy it. May you ever thank Him for enabling you to live within His tender care.

In the fifth month of pregnancy your baby's nostrils reopen and respiratory-like movements begin; your child is 6-7.28 inches long; the baby's movements are strong enough for you to feel. (Lowdermilk, 343). You are carrying a beautiful part of future generations in your womb today. How your Creator must delight in His creation, the sheep of His pasture!

Prayer
Dear God,
Thank You, Lord, for the masterpiece growing within me. I pray You will continue to watch over my child and me. Give me strength when I am weary and courage when I am faint-hearted. Let me rest securely as a sheep in your pasture. In Jesus' name, amen.

Song
August, Chris. "The Maker." *The Maker*. Word Entertainment. 2015. CD.

Week 21 Day 3

"Consider it pure joy, my brothers, whenever you face trials of many kinds, because you know that the testing of your faith develops perseverance. Perseverance must finish its work so that you may be mature and complete, not lacking anything…" (Jas. 1.2-4)

I was once asked if it was easier to carry twins or run a marathon. I quickly answered, "Run a marathon." The individual was surprised, until I explained that I could train for a predetermined distance, unlike pregnancy. My pregnancy changed my faith life forever. When your faith is tested, you truly grow in your relationship with God. One must persevere with God alone when the course is unknown and the finish line is clouded by human uncertainty. He has promised to give you strength when you need it and to help you through every moment. So remember "…blessed is the man who perseveres under trial, because when he has stood the test, he will receive the crown of life that God has promised to those who love him." (Jas. 1.12)

Prayer

Dear Lord,

Help me to finish the race. Give me the patience and strength I need to complete the tasks You have given me. Draw me closer to You as You lovingly enable me to persevere. Please watch over the gift growing within me. In Jesus' name, amen.

Song

Camp, Jeremy. "He Knows." *I Will Follow*. Sparrow Records, 2015. CD.

Week 21 Day 4

"Let them praise his name with dancing and make music to him with tambourine and harp. For the Lord takes delight in his people; he crowns the humble with salvation."
(Ps. 149.3-4)

During my pregnancy one of my sons would kick with delight as the music played in worship services, while the other son often saved his movements for the sermon. We laughed at the possibility of me carrying a future preacher and musician. Perhaps you can feel your baby dancing inside of you? During the fifth month your baby is more active and you can really feel the movements. Your child's brain is developing rapidly, and he is able to open his eyes. Now he is growing hair and has individual finger and toe prints. It's exciting to know even his lungs are formed, although not yet functioning. (American College of Obstetricians and Gynecologists, Web) As you cherish the activity and development of your baby, know that the Lord delights in both of you also. Make music to the Lord, the God of your salvation!

Prayer
Dear Jesus,
I know through Your atoning sacrifice we are forgiven and redeemed. Thank You for my salvation! May my child continue to dance within me and may I delight in her as You delight in me. In Jesus' name, amen.

Song
Chapman, Steven C. "Lord of the Dance." *Signs of Life*. Sparrow Records, 1996. CD.

Week 21 Day 5

"When I consider your heavens, the work of your fingers, the moon and the stars, which you have set in place, what is man that you are mindful of him, the son of man that you care for him?" (Ps. 8.3-4)

Have you ever gazed into the sunset or been immersed in the beautiful color of a quiet sunrise? I know God is pleased with His masterpiece and your admiration. It is humbling to know that the God of the universe is not only aware of your existence, but He is intimately involved in your world. He knows your comings and goings, your thoughts and desires, your joys and your sorrows. Your Amazing God cares about you! The same fingers that formed the moon and stars created your child. You are blessed beyond measure because God is mindful of you. When you look upon the sky God painted just for you, celebrate His great love for you and your child.

Prayer
Dear Creator,
Thank you for giving me a beautiful world to live in and the ability to carry life within me. Please remember my child and me. Keep my baby safe and help me to rest securely in Your mighty hand with the assurance of Your love. In Jesus' name, amen.

Song
Tomlin, Chris. "Indescribable." *Arriving*. Sparrow Records, 2004. CD.

Week 22 Day 1

"Does he who implanted the ear not hear? Does he who formed the eye not see? Does he who disciplines nations not punish? Does he who teaches man lack knowledge? The Lord knows the thoughts of man; he knows that they are futile. Blessed is the man you discipline, O Lord, the man you teach from your law; you grant him relief from days of trouble, till a pit is dug for the wicked. For the Lord will not reject his people; he will never forsake his inheritance…When I said, "My foot is slipping," your love, O Lord, supported me. When anxiety was great within me, your consolation brought joy to my soul." (Ps. 94.9-19)

It is easy to take for granted the incredible gift of sight until your ability to see is impaired. Now at six months your child can open and close his eyes! (American College of Obstetricians and Gynecologists, Web) Your vision allows you to see the world and interpret different stimuli. God, however, is not limited by human vision. He can perceive your child, your circumstances, and the deepest longings of your soul. God has promised to console and support you when your "…foot is slipping…" What a blessed assurance of His grace!

Prayer
Dear Lord,

Thank You for looking into my heart and caring for my deepest need. I know You preserve my life when I am falling. Please give me strength to carry this child and help her to see You as her loving Creator. In Jesus' name, amen.

Song
TobyMac. "Feel It." *This Is Not a Test*. Forefront, 2015. CD.

Week 22 Day 2

"Turn to me and have mercy on me; grant your strength to your servant and save the son of your maidservant."
(Ps. 86.16)

Do you long to lie down in the evenings and then yearn for the dawn when you can arise from your uncomfortable position? Is your strength gone and your spirit weary? Cry out to Jesus! He will grant you strength, just as He did with David in the psalm above. My Pastor once said that God will give you more than you can bear in the hopes that you will seek Him. God loves you and longs to be gracious to you. Turn to your Savior and ask for mercy. He will give you strength and peace beyond human understanding.

Prayer
Lord,
Please give me the strength I need to complete the work You given me. Help me to serve You with my life. If it is your will, Lord, enable my body to continue this pregnancy without complications. Help me to seek You fervently because I know that You will keep us close. In every circumstance, help me to surrender our lives to Your care. In Jesus' name, amen.

Song
Redman, Matt. "10,000 Reasons (Bless the Lord)." *10,000 Reasons*. Chordant Distribution Group, 2011. CD.

Week 22 Day 3

"I thank my God every time I remember you. In all my prayers for all of you, I always pray with joy because of your partnership in the gospel from the first day until now, being confident of this, that he who began a good work in you will carry it on to completion until the day of Christ Jesus." (Phil. 1.3-6)

He has begun "a good work in you…" by creating faith in your heart and a child in your womb. Therefore, thank God for the wonderful child growing inside of you and for the gift of eternal life. May God fill you with His Spirit as you lead your child to the one true Savior, Jesus Christ.

I look forward to the day in paradise when mothers will be reunited with the children God called home before them. For God has promised that "he who began a good work in you will carry it on to completion until the day of Christ Jesus." He will bring our salvation to completion in heaven. May we encourage those around us with Christ's love as we journey together towards our celestial home.

Prayer

Dear Christ Jesus,

Please continue to bless this "good work" You have begun in me. Let my heart be filled with Your Holy Spirit so I can continue on this journey faithfully. May this child thrive, and may I be a mother after Your own heart. Amen.

Song

Brewster, Lincoln. "Made New." *Oxygen*. Integrity, 2014. CD.

Week 22 Day 4

"Give thanks to the Lord, for he is good; his love endures forever." (1 Chron. 16.34)

As mothers we understand and demonstrate unconditional love that lasts forever. Our imperfect affections and intentions are only a glimpse of Christ's vast and perfect love. Let us demonstrate our gratefulness for the mercy our Savior gives, by granting forgiveness and love to our family, too.

"God sends children to enlarge our hearts and make us unselfish and full of kindly sympathies and affections."
-Mary Howitt

Prayer
Dearest Jesus,

Thank You for forgiving me for my terrible sins. Create in me a heart willing to love, cherish, and forgive my family. May I always show the same enduring love to this precious child of mine. Amen.

Song
Third Day. "You Are Good." *Offerings II: All I Have to Give.* Essential Records, 2003. CD.

Week 22 Day 5

"There, in the presence of the Lord your God, you and your families shall eat and shall rejoice in everything you have put your hand to, because the Lord your God has blessed you." (Deut.12.7)

Before you consume your meals, do you give thanks to your Heavenly Father for the food He has provided? It is tempting to view your food as a provision you prepared and earned, but God is the giver of all good things. He wants you to prepare your heart before you receive His blessings. As you plan for the arrival of one of your dearest blessings, give thanks to the Lord and then rejoice as you receive His gracious gift.

Prayer
Dear Jesus,

Thank You for providing my family with food and shelter. We are grateful for the opportunity to work and play. Your bountiful blessings fill our hearts with joy. Please watch over the precious gift of life growing inside of me. May he be strong in body, mind, and spirit as he grows into a man of God, according to Your will. Amen.

Song
Tomlin, Chris. "Holy Is the Lord." *Arriving*. Six Step Records, 2004. CD.

Week

23

Week 23 Day 1

"May the God of peace, who through the blood of the eternal covenant brought back from the dead our Lord Jesus, that great Shepherd of the sheep, equip you with everything good for doing his will, and may he work in us what is pleasing to him, through Jesus Christ, to whom be glory for ever and ever. Amen." (Heb.13.20)

Are you ready to be a mom to this baby? Do you feel capable and prepared? If so, rest in gratitude for the gift of confidence. At other times, when you are plagued with doubts and feelings of inadequacy, God tells you to rejoice. For He has promised to "…equip you with everything good for doing his will…." He will provide all that you need to care for your children. God has chosen you to be the mother of this little person, and He will continue to guide you in your endeavor to raise a God-fearing and God-loving individual.

Prayer

Dear Jesus,

Thank You for equipping me to be the mother You have called me to be. Forgive me for my doubts and imperfections. Help me to be mindful of the investment I must make in my child's future salvation and to rejoice in Your promise to prepare and equip me. Amen.

Song

Sidewalk Prophets. "Live Like That." *Live Like That*. Word Entertainment, 2012. CD.

Week 23 Day 2

"However, as it is written: "No eye has seen, no ear has heard, no mind has conceived what God has prepared for those who love him"-but God has revealed it to us by his Spirit." (1Cor. 2.9)

When I was pregnant with our first child, I was frequently told that a baby would change my life. I knew I would be sleep-deprived and responsible for another human being, but I did not fully understand the deep, sacrificial love that comes with motherhood. Later, during my twin pregnancy, I anticipated the work and effort parenting would involve. But I didn't expect the amplified joy that came with raising infants simultaneously. If watching one baby's antics is amusing, imagine witnessing a pair of babies giggling in response to their older sibling.

Certain aspects of those first few years were extremely difficult, but there were many magnified moments of delight. Sometimes during my pregnancy, it was difficult to perceive the happiness God had planned for our future because of the possible challenges tomorrow might bring. However, even on our hard days, we can take comfort in the knowledge that someday all our pain and suffering will disappear when we join our Heavenly Father in His kingdom.

Prayer

Dear Jesus,

 I don't know what my future holds, but I trust You with my life. Fill my heart with hope and let me look forward to the future with the joyful certainty of Your great plans for us. Please bless and protect my child as I await her arrival. Amen.

Song

Needtobreathe. "Multiplied." *Rivers in the Wasteland*. Atlantic Records, 2014. CD.

Week 23 Day 3

"As you do not know the path of the wind, or how the body is formed in a mother's womb, so you cannot understand the work of God, the Maker of all things." (Eccles. 11.5)

Have you ever been overwhelmed by the complexity of God's design in nature? If you consider how a leaf is able to change carbon dioxide to oxygen, it is awe inspiring. God's masterpiece consists of interdependent creations living independently, but thriving together. Everywhere you look in nature, you can see God's handiwork. The vibrant and beautiful colors of the autumn leaves are glimpses of God's love for His creation. He delights in you and your child. He loving fashioned you in His image and tenderly shaped your unborn baby with His plan in mind. God has a purpose for you and your child that you cannot fully understand. "Come and see what God has done, how awesome his works in man's behalf!" (Ps. 66.5)

Prayer

Loving Creator God,

Thank You for giving us this beautiful world to live in. It is inspiring to see the works of Your hand displayed in all their majesty. Thank You for creating this amazing child within my womb. Please watch over my baby and help him to grow according to Your will. Give me wisdom that I might understand Your will for my life. In Jesus' name, amen.

Song

Dixon, Colton. "You Are." *A Messenger*. Sparrow Records, 2013. CD.

Week 23 Day 4

"My frame was not hidden from you when I was made in the secret place. When I was woven together in the depths of the earth, your eyes saw my unformed body. All the days ordained for me were written in your book before one of them came to be." (Ps.139.15-16)

Although your baby is growing in darkness, concealed from the world, her Creator sees her and has ordained her days before they even begin. God knows how long your child will walk on the earth before her foot even touches the ground. He knows the number of days that will pass before you join Him in His heavenly dwelling too. God's omniscience is a comfort because He is our shepherd and our guide. He will lead us down paths of righteousness because He knows the way. Will you follow your Lord? When the future is uncertain, trust in God because He loves you and your child.

Song
Brandon Heath. "No Turning Back." *No Turning Back*. Provident Label Group, 2015. CD.

Week 23 Day 5

"She is clothed with strength and dignity; she can laugh at the days to come. She speaks with wisdom, and faithful instruction is on her tongue." (Prov. 31.25-26)

During the first year with twin boys, I learned to laugh at the days to come. Without laughter the future is intimidating. My husband knew that secret long before me; consequently, he was able to confidently say from the beginning, "It'll be fun!" regarding our high-risk pregnancy.

Children bring a new and meaningful perspective to life that transforms your inspirations and your aspirations. When you choose not to worry about the unknown, you can look forward to tomorrow with hope. For when you know who determines your future, you can calmly rest in Jesus' hand. Then, you can witness to others with wise and faithful words.

"Who shall set a limit to the influence of one human being?" -Ralph Waldo Emerson

Prayer

Lord,

Thank You for the tremendous, life-changing gift of this child. Help me to view the future with optimism. Allow me to thrive in the assurance of Your presence and to speak the truth of Your love to those around me. In Jesus' name, amen.

Song

Chapman, Steven C. "Love Take Me Over." *The Glorious Unfolding.* Reunion Records, 2013. CD,

Week 24 Day 1

"For since the creation of the world God's invisible qualities-his eternal power and divine nature-have been clearly seen, being understood from what has been made, so that men are without excuse." (Rom.1.20)

Consider the majestic mountains, the vast depths of the oceans, and the colors God paints in the sky every day. His handprints surround us as evidence of His divine power. May we stand in awe of His majesty and proclaim His glory.

Your baby is an incredible display of God's handiwork. Look at the spectacular changes your abdomen is making to enable you to bring forth a baby. Inside your womb, hidden from view, your child is undergoing astonishing development. Give thanks to the Lord, for He is good!

Prayer

Dear Lord,

I am captivated by the works of Your hand. I rejoice that I am filled with the blessing of Your creation. Let my heart and mouth always praise You, for You are amazing, God. In Jesus' name, amen.

Song

Newsboys. "He Reigns." *Adoration: The Worship Album.* Sparrow Records, 2003. CD.

Week 24 Day 2

"And they sang a new song: "You are worthy to take the scroll and to open its seals, because you were slain, and with your blood you purchased men for God from every tribe and language and people and nation." (Rev. 5.9)

Christ's sacrificial death was necessary for your salvation. His precious blood cleanses you from all unrighteousness and allows you to stand before God with complete forgiveness. In the Old Testament the blood of an animal was sometimes referred to as its "lifeblood." In this sixth month, your child's own blood formation is increasing, enabling her to receive the oxygen and the vital nutrients she needs to thrive. (U.S. National Library of Medicine, Web)

May your child join in a new song of thanksgiving for Christ's atoning sacrifice.

Prayer

Precious Savior,

Thank You for sacrificing Your life for me. I am eternally grateful, and I pray You will cover my child with Your precious blood of forgiveness. Forgive me for nailing You to the cross with my sins. Thank You for loving me enough to die for my baby and me! May we ever praise you! Amen.

Song

Big Daddy Weave. "Redeemed." *Love Come to Life*. Fervent Records, 2012. CD.

Week 24 Day 3

"Surely he will never by shaken; a righteous man will be remembered forever. He will have no fear of bad news; his heart is steadfast, trusting in the Lord." (Ps.112.6-7)

As women we set the tone for the home. When we are encouraging and happy, the family usually follows our example. However, if we are unhappy, stressed, or angry we can see our attitudes reflected in our loved ones. I know none of us are perfect, especially me. Yet, it is our responsibility to make our home a loving environment. Therefore, surround yourself with the words of your loving Savior. Be restored by the promise of His forgiveness and bestow the gift of forgiveness on those around you. Lay your burdens of anxiety at the foot of the cross so your heart may be "…steadfast, trusting in the Lord…"

Prayer
Dear God,
Thank You for giving me the opportunity to manage a home. Please help me to create a loving and nurturing dwelling for my children and spouse. Forgive me when I sin against those dearest to me and renew a right spirit within me. Help me to trust You with my child and my life. In Jesus' name, amen.

Song
One Sonic Society. "Never Once." *One Sonic Society*. Essential Records, 2013. CD.

Week 24 Day 4

"The Lord delights in those who fear him, who put their hope in his unfailing love." (Ps. 147.11)

The world considers independence and self-reliance when judging a person's success. God however, looks at a woman's heart and praises the woman who doesn't place her confidence solely in herself to obtain blessings. God wants you to respect Him as your sovereign Lord and to trust in His unfailing love. Imperfect human beings can disappoint us, but your Heavenly Father will always provide and always sustain the woman who puts her hope in Him.

Prayer

Dear Lord,

It is easy for me to be deceived into believing my individual efforts will bring me happiness, but I know You are the giver of all good things. Thank You for blessing my life beyond measure and for the gift of this baby. Help me to trust in You completely and to kneel before You as the Lord of my life. In Jesus' name, amen.

Song

David Crowder Band. "Wholly Yours." *A Collision*. Six Step Records, 2005. CD.

Week 24 Day 5

"Then, because so many people were coming and going that they did not even have a chance to eat, he (Jesus) said to them, "Come with me by yourselves to a quiet place and get some rest." (Mark 6.31)

Look at what an enchanting invitation Jesus offers to His disciples when He bids them, "Come with me by yourselves to a quiet place and get some rest." Jesus is giving you the same opportunity. If you have been confined to bed rest, I would encourage you to view this as a time of intimate fellowship with the Creator of your heart and your baby. God loves you both and He enjoys your company!

Prayer
Dear Jesus,

Help me to look forward to this time of rest. I know it will be good for my soul to commune with You. Let this time of dedication enable my child to grow within the safety of my womb. Please grant me joy and patience during this time of waiting. Amen.

Song
Dixon, Colton. "Through All of It." *Anchor.* Sparrow, 2014. CD.

Week 25 Day 1

"Finally, be strong in the Lord and in his mighty power. Put on the full armor of God so that you can take your stand against the devil's schemes." (Eph. 6.10)

Without the help of the Lord, it is difficult to face the challenges of a sinful world. We are unprepared and unable to withstand the attacks Satan makes against us when we battle alone. That is why God dresses us in His armor. He gives us the protection we need to face the "devil's schemes" through the Bible, prayer, and the Holy Spirit. "This week, let us explore in God's Word how we can train our hearts and minds to be soldiers of the cross and champions of faith for our children.

Prayer
Dear Lord,
Help me to find my protection in You. Cover me with Your armor, strengthen me with Your power, and lead me in this life. Thank You for not leaving me defenseless in this fallen world and for sending Your Son to save me. In Jesus' name. Amen.

Song
Jobe, Kari. "Alone." *Majestic.* Sparrow, 2014. CD.

Week 25 Day 2

"Stand firm then, with the belt of truth buckled around your waist, with the breastplate of righteousness in place, and with your feet fitted with the readiness that comes from the gospel of peace." (Eph. 6.14-15)

In this passage a soldier's character is his best defense, not his physical strength. The Lord equips His warriors with His armor so they will not be vulnerable to every attack from the enemy. God also clothes us with the breastplate of Christ's righteousness to guard our hearts. He does not want us to be overcome with the sorrows of sin and the arrows of guilt Satan can launch. In His wisdom, God enables us to "Above all else, guard your heart, for it is the wellspring of life." (Prov. 4.23) The belt of truth is the symbolic clothing of the Messiah in Isaiah. "Righteousness will be his belt and faithfulness the sash around his waist." (Isa. 11.5) Even when we feel we are facing the world alone, Christ is protecting us and holding us together. The gospel of Christ supports us and makes us ready to move where the Spirit leads us. Take heart! God is preparing you for motherhood and the world.

Prayer
Dear Jesus,

I long for Your protection. Prepare my mind and soul to face the enemy. Thank you for covering me with your righteousness. Help me to stand faithfully with You knowing You are watching over my baby. Amen.

Song
Rend Collective. "You Will Never Run." *As Family We Go.* Rend Collective, 2015. CD.

Week 25 Day 3

"In addition to all this, take up the shield of faith, with which you can extinguish all the flaming arrows of the evil one." (Eph. 6.15)

According to the footnotes in the Concordia Self-Study Bible, the shield described above was a "...large Roman shield covered with leather, which could be soaked in water and used to put out flame-tipped arrows." (Hoerber, 1812) This imagery reminds me of our baptism. Through baptism, God washes away our sins and fills us with the Holy Spirit. The power of the Holy Spirit living in us then makes it possible for us to withstand the devil's ruthless attacks. Faith is a shield that can defend us against many adversaries, including fear, pain, suffering, and loss. When you raise your child up in faith, you are protecting her from the evils in this world and equipping her with the armor of God.

Prayer
Dear Lord,
Thank You for creating faith in my heart and empowering me with the Holy Spirit. Help me to lead my child to You, so that she may be protected by Your armor of faith. Please watch over her as she grows and keep her safe. In Jesus' name, amen.

Song
Unspoken. "Good Fight." *Unspoken*. Centricity Music, 2014. CD.

Week 25 Day 4

"Take the helmet of salvation and the sword of the Spirit, which is the word of God." (Eph. 6.17)

My husband enjoys using large machinery and working on equipment. He also likes clearing trees and doing various outdoor tasks. So whenever he asks for my assistance in a job I don't feel comfortable doing, I jokingly ask, "Do I need my helmet for this?" He finds my bright orange helmet that usually sits off-center on my head amusing. When we are using old tractors to unload broken-down bulldozers from trailers, or dropping large trees, my crooked hard hat gives me a sense of security.

Our knowledge of our Savior is our helmet of protection in this world. The promise of our eternal salvation allows us to face earthly challenges fearlessly because we know that the battle for our souls has already been won.

Prayer
Dear Jesus,

Thank You for the joy of my salvation. Help me to face every obstacle with courage because I know I will spend eternity with You. Watch over my child as he grows and keep him in Your loving protection.

Song
Tomlin, Chris. "Forever." *The Noise We Make.* Sparrow Records, 2001. CD.

Week 25 Day 5

"Take the helmet of salvation and the sword of the Spirit, which is the word of God." (Eph. 6.17)

After Halloween I found two fabulously ornate, plastic pirate swords on clearance. I was slightly apprehensive about bringing them home to my 5-year-old boys, but they looked so fun! When I showed them to my husband, he quickly exclaimed, "Where's mine?"

Although we may not all be aggressive, I would presume most people would prefer having a sword, as well a shield, if they were ever in combat. God calls the Bible, "...the sword of the Spirit..." His word is powerful! We can use it to cut through the fallacies of this world and the lies of Satan. When we immerse ourselves in scripture, we are training ourselves for battle and sharpening our swords.

Prayer

Dear God,

Thank You for the gift of Your word. Help me as I study the Bible to discern what Your words truly mean. Let me use the power of the sword of the Spirit to defend against Satan's lies. Fill my heart with Your promises. Thank You for protecting my baby and me during my pregnancy. In Jesus' name, amen.

Song

MercyMe. "Word of God Speak." *Spoken For.* Columbia, 2002. CD.

Week 26 Day 1

"And pray in the Spirit on all occasions with all kinds of prayers and requests. With this in mind, be alert and always keep on praying for all the saints." (Eph. 6.18)

Now that you are dressed in the armor of God, "...be alert and always keep on praying..." The blessing of prayer is yours through the Holy Spirit. God wants you to fervently seek Him in everything. He longs to be a part of your life. You are encouraged to pray for all believers and your child each day. Ask your Heavenly Father to help your child grow healthy and strong. Do not be afraid to boldly present your requests to God or to humbly beseech Him for restoration. God is with you on all occasions.

Prayer
Dear God,
Thank You for listening to all of my requests and for hearing all my prayers. Please help my child to thrive. I trust in Your promises and pray that Your will be done. May my heart always follow You. In Jesus' name, amen.

Song
Grant, Amy. "Better Than a Hallelujah." *Somewhere Down the Road.* AGG, 2010. CD.

Week 26 Day 2

"I am the vine; you are the branches. If a man remains in me and I in him, he will bear much fruit; apart from me you can do nothing." (John 15.5)

Your relationship with Christ means everything. He is there to help you fulfill your purpose and enable you to "...bear much fruit..." God has opened your womb and allowed you to carry this child. May He continue you to bless you during your pregnancy. Take courage in knowing God is the source of your life and your child's. He breathed life into your baby and He is sustaining you through this pregnancy. Trust in Jesus and watch what amazing things you can accomplish together.

Prayer

Dear Jesus,

Thank You for giving me life and for creating this life inside of me. Help my baby grow stronger with every passing day. May we always remain in Your love and live our lives to bring You glory. In Jesus' name, amen.

Song

Gray, Jason. "Remind Me Who I Am." *Remind Me Who I Am.* Centricity Music, 2011. CD.

Week 26 Day 3

"If you remain in me and my words remain in you, ask whatever you wish, and it will be given you. This is to my Father's glory, that you bear much fruit, showing yourselves to be my disciples. "As the Father has loved me, so have I loved you. Now remain in my love." (John 15.7-9)

Jesus is inviting you to remain in His love so that He may show you the same tenderness the Heavenly Father has shown Him. Christ suffered and died on the cross for the sins of the world. God raised Him from the dead and now He sits in glory on His heavenly throne. He prepares a place for you there with no tears or suffering because Christ has overcome death. If you hold onto His love and believe He is your Savior, then you will spend eternity with Him in heaven.

Christ wants you to be known as His follower by your faith. He claims you as His own and encourages you to read the scriptures so that you may know His will. Then present your requests to the God who longs to be gracious to you. He is your loving Savior.

Prayer

Dear Jesus,

Thank You for Your love and faithfulness. Keep me in the faith and help me to share Your love with my baby. Draw us near to You until we come to live with You in Heaven. Please fill my heart with Your words and grant my prayers and petitions according to Your great mercy.

Song

Shust, Aaron. "Watch Over Me." *Doxology*. Centricity Music, 2007. CD.

Week 26 Day 4

"I have told you this so that my joy may be in you and that your joy may be complete. My command is this: Love each other as I have loved you. Greater love has no one than this, that he lay down his life for his friends." (John 15.11-13)

God wants you to be happy in this life because you have the promise of a heavenly home. Right now as you are growing this precious child, possibly on restricted activity, you are laying down your life for this child. You are temporarily sacrificing your individual desires for the well-being of this child. There is no greater love. Christ cherished you enough to surrender His life for you and your child. Now you can continue to share Christ's amazing love with this child and those around you. Rejoice, for Jesus loves you and your precious baby!

Prayer
Dear Lord,
I rejoice in my salvation and the gift of this baby. Please watch over her and keep her safe in Your hands. Help me to see this time of rest as a gift and a blessing. Please use it to grow my beloved baby. In Jesus' name, amen.

Song
Wickham, Phil. "This Is Amazing Grace." *The Ascension*. Fair Trade, 2013. CD.

Week 26 Day 5

"Teach us to number our days aright, that we may gain a heart of wisdom." (Ps. 90.12)

Your days on earth are few and your days on bed rest are even fewer. Although they may seem excruciatingly long, they are numbered. How can this time of inactivity and confinement help you "...gain a heart of wisdom..." during your pregnancy? Will you study God's word, spend time in prayer, or make plans for motherhood? God knows you and where you are. He has allowed you to endure these circumstances because He has a purpose in mind for you. May God give you the strength and patience necessary to enjoy your days of rest as you anticipate your future blessings. Congratulations on making it through your second trimester!

Prayer

Dear Jesus,

The days on bed rest seem so much longer! Help me to remember that these days are limited. Give me a heart that desires to find fellowship with you throughout this pregnancy. Draw me closer and please keep my baby safe in Your loving care. Make me ever mindful of the blessing growing stronger within me with each passing day. Amen.

Song

Gray, Jason. "Remind Me Who I Am." *A Way to See in the Dark.* EMI Gospel, 2011. CD.

3rd Trimester

Week
27

Week 27 Day 1

"Do you not know? Have you not heard? The Lord is the everlasting God, the Creator of the ends of the earth. He will not grow tired or weary, and his understanding no one can fathom. He gives strength to the weary and increases the power of the weak. Even youths grow tired and weary, and young men stumble and fall; but those who hope in the Lord will renew their strength. They will soar on wings like eagles; they will run and not grow weary, they will walk and not be faint." (Isa. 40.28-31)

Can you imagine what it would be like to never be exhausted? Right now, your body is growing and sustaining a tiny miracle. It's no wonder you are tired! God's strength, however, never fades and He doesn't need time to recuperate. Moreover, He is willing to bestow His strength upon you because of His bountiful love and compassion. God can lift up your spirit in the midst of the most difficult circumstances. When you are fatigued by your temporal obligations and situation, take time to seek the Lord's help. He faithfully replenishes your body so you can continue to nurture your baby. Congratulations, you're in the third trimester!

Prayer
Dearest Savior,
Please give me the strength I need to carry this baby until the day he arrives. Restore my soul for You are the source of all my hope. Amen.

Song
Tomlin, Chris. "Everlasting God." *See the Morning*. Six Step Records, 2006. CD.

Week 27 Day 2

"He tends his flock like a shepherd; He gathers the lambs in his arms and carries them close to his heart; he gently leads those that have young." (Isa. 40.11)

Even as you guide your own children through life, you are still dependent on the gracious and tender care of Jesus. You will always be Jesus' little lamb. Ultimately, you trust Him to lead you because He has been faithful before. He knows where streams of water flow, safe from the threat of this world's dangers. The Bible says He is actively involved in your life because "...He tends his flock like a shepherd..." He will not leave you to find your way alone. He bids you to follow Him through the darkness. And when you are unable to follow, He will carry you close to His heart. Especially now, when you have a young one growing within you and the path is sometimes uncertain, He gathers you into His loving arms.

Prayer

Dear Jesus, My Shepherd,

Thank You for faithfully guiding me through my life. Help me to follow You down this road and to rest assured that You always remember my little lamb and me. Amen.

Song

Tenth Avenue North. "By Your Side." *Over and Underneath.* Reunion Records, 2008. CD.

Week 27 Day 3

"The Lord is my rock, my fortress and my deliverer; my God is my rock, in whom I take refuge. He is my shield and the horn of my salvation, my stronghold." (Ps. 18.2)

Have you ever been amazed by the enduring presence of an old fireplace in the midst of rubble or a vacant field? Even when your life seems to be a broken pile of troubles, God stands firm. He is Your rock foundation. The Lord is your stronghold; a place of security and steadfast fortification. He has promised to be your shield and salvation. So as you approach this new beginning as a mother, remember "...in whom I take refuge..." You need not be afraid. Your child is resting securely in the mighty hands of your Savior.

Prayer
Lord Jesus, My Rock,
Thank You for being my stronghold through this journey. Please continue to protect and sustain me during this lengthy journey. Please shield my child from all that would harm her and help me to take refuge in You. Amen.

Song
Third Day. "Trust In Jesus." *Move.* Essential Records, 2010. CD.

Week 27 Day 4

"Nehemiah said, "Go and enjoy choice food and sweet drinks, and send some to those who have nothing prepared. This day is sacred to our Lord. Do not grieve, for the joy of the Lord is your strength." (Neh. 8.10)

This passage from the book of Nehemiah describes God's response to the Israelites' sorrow as they listened to the words of the Law. They were overwhelmed by their sinfulness, but God commanded His people to celebrate the Feast of Tabernacles. Once they repented, the Lord did not want His people to continue weeping. He wanted them to have joy for "...they now understood the words that had been made known to them..." (Neh. 8.12)

Regardless of your struggles and suffering on this earth, if you believe in Jesus as your Lord and Savior, you will one day live forever with your King and Creator. God wants you to celebrate as well because He has redeemed you and blessed you with a new life! May the Lord strengthen you with His love and fill your heart with joy.

Prayer

Precious Jesus,

Thank You for revealing Yourself to me. Please create a living faith in my child and help me to share the joy of salvation with those around me. May we rest happily in Your love. Amen.

Song

Paris, Twila. "The Joy of the Lord." *Sanctuary*. Star Song Music, 1991. CD.

Week 27 Day 5

"All Scripture is God-breathed and is useful for teaching, rebuking, correcting and training in righteousness, so that the man of God may be thoroughly equipped for every good work." (2 Tim. 3.16)

Have you ever been captivated by the words of a verse that directly applies to your present situation? During those times God's intimate knowledge of you and your life is almost incomprehensible. Meditating on the passages in God's word will keep you "...thoroughly equipped for every good work..." Motherhood and pregnancy require spiritual preparation and refreshment. Later, when you have parenting questions and concerns, God's word is a guide for raising a child in the faith and admonition of the Lord. He has given you authority over your children and has commanded children to obey their parents. God wants you to study His word and to teach the scriptures to your children, so that together your family will be prepared to complete the tasks God has planned.

Prayer
Dear Heavenly Father,
The idea of becoming a Mom and being responsible for another person is sometimes very intimidating. Help me to remember that You have promised to equip me for the work involved in motherhood. Please help me to trust in You to guide me as a parent. Watch over my precious child and keep her safe. In Jesus' name, amen.

Song
Plumb. "Don't Deserve You." *Need You Now*. Curb Records, 2013. CD.

Week
28

Week 28 Day 1

"Finally, be strong in the Lord and in his mighty power."
(Eph. 6.10)

When I venture out on errands people often exclaim,
"You have your hands full!" When I am feeling courageous I
will respond, "Full of blessings." Shamefully, there have been
times when I have not always been "...prepared to give an
answer to everyone who asks you to give the reason for the
hope that you have. But do this with gentleness and respect,
keeping a clear conscience..." (1 Pet. 3.15-16) During those
times I have averted my eyes from the curious glances and
kept my focus on temporal things, rather than perceiving the
world through the light of Christ. My prayer is that you will
draw your strength from the Lord and willingly proclaim it.
God bountifully blesses you when you acknowledge Him as
the source of your good fortune.

Prayer

Dear Lord,
Thank You for giving me strength when I am weary.
Please help me to cling to You and to confess that You are my
strength, my Savior, and my Lord. Forgive me when I deny
You the honor You deserve. In Jesus' name, amen.

Song

Hillsong Church. "You Are My Strength." *Saviour King.*
Hillsong, 2007. CD.

Week 28 Day 2

"Therefore my heart is glad and my tongue rejoices; my body also will rest secure, because you will not abandon me to the grave, nor will you let your Holy One see decay. You have made known to me the path of life; you will fill me with joy in your presence." (Ps. 16.9-11)

Even on bed rest your heart can be filled with joy because you appreciate the miracle growing inside of you. Let gladness consume you because you are resting in the gracious provision of your Heavenly Father. God has revealed to you the joy of your salvation and the promise of eternity. Now, as you take refuge during this time of waiting and anticipation, rejoice that God cares for you and your child. He knows when you wake and sleep and rest. He is with you every moment of every day. May you find peace and comfort in His presence.

Prayer

Dear Heavenly Father,

Thank You for watching over my baby and me as we wait for the wonderful day of his birth. Grant me the repose I need to help him grow healthy and strong. Let me remain securely in Your grasp and help me trust in Your promise to always be with us. In Jesus' name, amen.

Song

Grace, Jamie. "You Lead." *Ready to Fly*. Gotee Records, 2014. CD.

Week 28 Day 3

"But he answered one of them, 'Friend, I am not being unfair to you. Didn't you agree to work for a denarius? Take your pay and go. I want to give the man who was hired last the same as I gave you. Don't I have the right to do what I want with my own money? Or are you envious because I am generous?" (Matt. 20.13-15)

How many times have we heard or said, "That's not fair!" or asked, "Why?" with bitterness in our hearts? Even at a young age, we understand when someone has something we desire or more than our share. We want life to be fair, but reality is often contrary to this ideology. Honestly, if God gave us what we deserved, we would be in a miserable state. The punishment of sin is death, yet because of His great mercy and love God sent His only Son to die in our place as payment for our sins. God graciously chose to offer His own Son in our stead. I could not fathom giving up my child to save a sinner. Could you? But that is how much God loves you! No matter how angry you are with God or how unfair your baby's condition seems, remember that God loves you both. In His great mercy, He offered Himself up for you as a living sacrifice. God does not make mistakes, and He does not promise we will always understand His will. However, He does promise to never leave you, nor forsake you. Hold onto your Savior, and He will carry you through this.

Prayer
Dear Jesus,

Thank you for dying on the cross for my most grievous sins. When my heart is full of anger and bitterness, please cleanse my soul and fill me again with your loving spirit. Heal my heart and remind me of how much You love me. Wrap me in Your forgiving arms of mercy and help me to understand Your will. Help me to accept Your plan for my baby's life and mine. Let me see Your beauty in the midst of this trial. Amen.

Song
Tomlin, Chris. "Your Grace Is Enough." *Arriving.* Six Steps Records, 2004. CD

Week 28 Day 4

"Now faith is being sure of what we hope for and certain of what we do not see." (Heb. 11:1)

The Holy Spirit is often compared to the wind because we claim it exists without being able to see it. We are certain of its presence because we can feel the effects and see its impact in the world around us. Leaves rustle, trees sway, water ripples, and birds soar. Through faith, we are certain God is alive and that His kingdom is near. We can feel the presence of God and see the work of the Holy Spirit in the lives of those around us. All creation testifies to His sovereignty.

Soon, you will hold the one hidden inside of you. As you feel the precious movements growing stronger within you, anticipate the day of your child's arrival with hope and faith. Surely that spectacular moment when you behold your child will encourage you to await Christ's second coming with renewed enthusiasm and joy.

Prayers

Dear Jesus,

I look forward to the day You bring me home. Help me to look upon my future with a hope built on Your promises. Please watch over the one only You can see as I feel her movements growing stronger.

In Jesus' name, amen.

Song

Mercyme. "I Can Only Imagine." *Almost There.* INO/EPIC, 2001. CD.

Week 28 Day 5

"Your attitude should be the same as that of Christ Jesus: Who, being in very nature God, did not consider equality with God something to be grasped, but made himself nothing, taking the very nature of a servant, being made in human likeness. And being found in appearance as a man, he humbled himself and became obedient to death even death on a cross! Therefore God exalted him to the highest place and gave him the name that is above every name, that at the name of Jesus every knee should bow, in heaven and under the earth, and every tongue confess that Jesus Christ is Lord, to the glory of God the Father." (Phil. 2.4-11)

At 7 months, your baby's eyes can open and close, he can kick, and make grasping motions with his tiny hands. (American College of Obstetricians and Gynecologists, Web)

Jesus relinquished His grasp on His heavenly position when He humbled Himself and became human. He laid aside His glory in order to live a perfect life. Jesus became the sacrificial lamb for the sins of the whole world. What are you holding onto that God is asking you to release? Is it fear, worry, anger, or unforgiveness? Let go, and let God fill your heart and your hands with His blessings instead.

Prayer
Dear Jesus,
Thank You for surrendering Your life for me and saving me from my sins. I can only imagine the glory You forfeited for me. Help me to surrender …. Amen.

Song
Sidewalk Prophets. "You Love Me Anyway." *These Simple Truths.* Fervent Records, 2009. CD.

Week 29 Day 1

"He has made everything beautiful in his time. He has also set eternity in the hearts of men; yet they cannot fathom what God has done from beginning to end." (Eccles. 3.11)

When you are in the midst of a difficult pregnancy, it is natural to want to understand God's plan for your child and your life. Often with the passing of time you can clearly see God's design in your circumstances. In other situations, God's reasoning is a mystery. In those moments rest assured, "...all the ways of the Lord are loving and faithful..." (Ps. 25.10). The Lord your God is always with you. Even when you cannot grasp all that God has done for you, abide in His grace. He has a plan for you although you cannot comprehend it. His intricate design is bringing together all the joys and sorrows of your life in a beautiful testimony of His love.

Prayer

Dear Lord,

Teach me Your ways. Help me to rest securely in Your will and to be confident of Your benevolent concern for my child and me. Forgive me when I try to force my will and to control all of my future. Make me mindful of Your beautiful design in my life and my child's. In Jesus' name, amen.

Song

Gungor. "Beautiful Things." *Beautiful Things.* Brash Records, 2010. CD.

Week 29 Day 2

"Surely God is my salvation; I will trust and not be afraid. The Lord, the Lord, is my strength and my song; he has become my salvation." (Isa. 12.2)

Look how far the Lord has brought you and this child! Soon you will see the beautiful creation God is growing in your womb. May your lips sing praises as you draw your strength from your Savior. He will continue to uphold you for you are never out of His grasp. Even in the most intimidating circumstances, God promises to never abandon you. Let your heart be filled with joy, as you rest in the assurance of God's mercy and your salvation.

Prayer
Dear Jesus,

I rejoice in Your promises and Your presence. My heart is glad because I know You are with me every day and that You will keep us in Your love forever. Thank You for being my strength and my salvation. Amen.

Song
MercyMe. "Greater." *Welcome to the New.* Fair Trade/Columbia, 2014. CD.

Week 29 Day 3

"We wait in hope for the Lord; he is our help and our shield. In him our hearts rejoice, for we trust in his holy name. May your unfailing love rest upon us, O Lord, even as we put our hope in you." (Ps. 33.20-22)

One morning on the radio I heard a woman's story regarding her unexpected and unfavorable ultrasound results, and it moved me to tears. She described her experience and the anguish she and her husband had felt that day. As she lay on the examination table, she stated confidently, "My Jesus is the same as He was before I walked in this room." She confessed with her mouth what she believed in her heart. This remarkable woman knew Jesus loved her and promised to be faithful in every circumstance. Although He did not promise a life without sorrow or suffering, He pledges "…so I will be with you; I will never leave you nor forsake you." (Joshua 1:5) This promise gives us hope in the midst of crisis and joy during life's celebrations.

Prayer
Dear Lord,
May the Holy Spirit fill my heart with the blessed assurance of Your constant and unfailing love. Forgive me when I fail to trust in You and help me to cling to Your promises. Watch over my precious child and keep us both within Your grasp. In Jesus' name, amen.

Song
Tomlin, Chris. "Jesus Loves Me." *Jesus Loves Me*. Six Step Records, 2015. CD.

Week 29 Day 4

"For we are God's workmanship, created in Christ Jesus to do good works, which God prepared in advance for us to do." (Eph. 2.10)

God has great plans for you for "'No eye has seen, no ear has heard, no mind has conceived what God has prepared for those who love him.'"-but God has revealed it to us by His Spirit. The Spirit searches all things, even the deep things of God." (2 Cor. 2.9-10) You have the privilege of mothering this precious gift from God. It will be work, but your efforts will be greatly rewarded. God loves moms! He knows the challenges you face, and He invites you to find your strength in Him. He gives you this precious blessing and promises to faithfully assist you in raising your child. So embrace your identity and responsibility courageously, for you are not alone.

A mother's love is like the tree of life.
Strong in spirit,
Peaceful, wise, and beautiful.
-American proverb

Prayer
Heavenly Father,
May my life be a blessing to this child, Lord. Help me to blossom into the mother You have created me to be so that I may lead this child into Your loving arms. In Jesus' name, amen.

Song
Maclean, Dara. "Wanted." *Wanted.* Fervent Records, 2013. CD.

Week 29 Day 5

"I will consider all your works and meditate on all your mighty deeds." Your ways, God, are holy. What god is as great as our God? You are the God who performs miracles; you display your power among the peoples. With your mighty arm you redeemed your people, the descendants of Jacob and Joseph." (Ps. 77.12-15)

In a world where responsibilities and schedules keep us focused on temporal things, it is important to remember our story as children of our Heavenly Father. Remember the Bible stories that describe how God saved His people from slavery, sin, and destruction. Contemplate the incredible love and mercy He showed by dying on the cross to save us. Dwell on the times when God has faithful in your life and rejoice. For He still performs miracles because our God reigns. May your life tell the story of Christ's amazing love.

Prayer
Dear Lord,

Please hear the pleas of my heart. Help me to focus on You and not this worldly life. Thank You for listening to my every word and for loving my baby and me. I am grateful for all the times you have rescued me with Your mighty hand. May we abide in Your gracious love and mercy forever. In Jesus' name, amen.

Song
Nichols, Morgan Harper. "The Storyteller." *Morgan Harper Nichols.* Gotee Records, 2015. CD.

Week 30 Day 1

"Do you know when the mountain goats give birth? Do you watch when the doe bears her fawn? Do you count the months till they bear? Do you know the time they give birth? They crouch down and bring forth their young; their labor pains are ended. Their young thrive and grow strong..." (Job 39.1-4)

During my high-risk pregnancy, this was the passage I treasured most. Here in these words, God revealed His great concern and affection for me, His creation. If He cares enough about the deer and mountain goats to "...count the months till they bear...," how much more concern does He have for you? You are always in His thoughts, and He is fully aware of the child growing inside of you. He is sovereign and powerful, but He truly and tenderly loves you and your child. Rest in His tender care as you await the day He has appointed for your child to arrive.

Prayer
Dearest Jesus,
"What is man that you are mindful of him..." (Ps. 8.4) Thank You for remembering my child and me. Please give me peace as the arrival of my child draws closer. In Jesus' name, amen.

Song
MercyMe. "Here with Me." *Undone*. Fair Trade Services, 2004. CD.

Week 30 Day 2

"I know that you can do all things; no plan of yours can be thwarted...Surely I spoke of things I did not understand, things too wonderful for me to know." (Job 42.2)

This passage deals with the biblical character of Job and his response to God after many, many trials had befallen him. Through the story of Job, God ensures us that He does not allow us to suffer without purpose. Even when His divine will is not revealed to us, we must trust in our gracious Heavenly Father to do what is necessary to accomplish His purpose.

After Job endured great heartache and loss, God blessed Him more abundantly. He did not abandon Job during his crisis. Your Heavenly Father is aware of the hard times you experience in this imperfect world, and He uses those opportunities to draw you closer to Him and to reveal His glory. Even when His ways are uncertain and life is difficult, do not doubt that God loves you.

Prayer

Dear Jesus,

Sometimes trusting in Your will is so hard! Grant me the faith I need to walk with You. Give me hope in a future only You can know and peace in the present. In Jesus' name. Amen.

Song

Roberts, Kerrie. "No Matter What." *Kerrie Roberts*. Reunion Records, 2010. CD.

Week 30 Day 3

"…The Lord is near. Do not be anxious about anything, but in everything, by prayer and petition, with thanksgiving present your requests to God. And the peace of God, which transcends all understanding will guard your hearts and your minds in Christ Jesus." (Phil. 4.4-7)

The opposite of anxiety is peace. God beseeches you to give Him your worries in exchange for the "…peace of God, which transcends all understanding…" It is tempting to allow your fears to consume you when you are unable to control the future. Yet, God calls you to surrender your will and your control. He promises to be near and to guard your heart and mind with His peace. Focus on the unchanging, loving God you have because He promises to be faithful.

Prayer
Dear Jesus,

I lay my burden down at Your feet and I ask You to carry me through this delivery. I know You understand my suffering and You know my need for a Savior. Please watch over my child and me as I face this exciting and intimidating time. Amen.

Song
Crowder, David. "Come As You Are." *Neon Steeple*. Six Step Records, 2014. CD.

Week 30 Day 4

"Yet you brought me out of the womb; you made me trust in you even at my mother's breast. From birth I was cast upon you; from my mother's womb you have been my God…" (Ps. 22.9-10)

In this psalm David testifies to God's influence in his life from the very beginning. Isn't that amazing? God has brought you though this life, and He will be there when your child comes into this world. He is aware of every circumstance and graciously holds you in His hand through every trial and miracle. Let your heart and voice declare His praise.

I was there to hear your borning cry,
I'll be there when you are old.
I rejoiced the day you were baptized,
to see your life unfold…

In the middle ages of your life,
not too old, no longer young,
I'll be there to guide you through the night,
complete what I've begun.

-John C. Ylvasiker

Prayer

Dear Jesus,

   I thank You for being my God and my sustainer. Help me to trust in You and Your faithfulness. Please surround my family and me during the birth of this child. Help me to feel Your presence as we begin this new chapter of our lives. Amen.

Song

August, Chris. "The Maker." *The Maker*. Fervent Records, 2015. CD.

Week 30 Day 5

"She sets about her work vigorously; her arms are strong for her tasks." (Prov. 31.17)

If you want to learn where your strength comes from, have twins. Within a few months of your pregnancy you will be keenly aware of your dependency on a faithful Heavenly Father and your personal limitations. There are times when I forget my source of strength, and I set about my tasks reliant on my own energy and will. It is during these moments that I realize how incapable I am of being independent. I need God's help and you will too. Be assured that "I can do everything through him who gives me strength." (Phil. 4.13) As you plan your new life, remember to ask for God's help and strength to complete the tasks He has given you.

Prayer
God of Power and of Strength,
Strengthen me on this exciting journey. I know I can do all things pleasing to You with Your help. Let me feel Your presence and power in my life. I come before You in prayer asking You to renew and sustain me. Please enable my child to continue to grow in safety and good health. In Jesus' name, amen.

Song
West, Matthew. "Strong Enough." *The Story of Your Life.* Sparrow Records, 2010. CD.

Week 31 Day 1

"Furious with rage, Nebuchadnezzar summoned Shadrach, Meshach and Abednego. So these men were brought before the king, and Nebuchadnezzar said to them, "Is it true, Shadrach, Meshach and Abednego, that you do not serve my gods or worship the image of gold I have set up? Now when you hear the sound of the horn, flute, zither, lyre, harp, pipes and all kind of music, if you are ready to fall down and worship the image I made, very good. But if you do not worship it, you will be thrown immediately into a blazing furnace. Then what god will be able to rescue you from my hand?" (Dan. 3.13-15)

As you approach your day of delivery it will be necessary for you to stand firm in your faith. You must believe that no matter what happens, God is with you through it all. He will bring this pregnancy to completion. What you are about to endure may seem as formidable as a blazing furnace, but do not be dismayed. You will soon learn "...what god will be able to rescue you..." in all things and in all circumstances great and small. He is always with you and your child.

Prayer
Dear Jesus,
    Delivery is scary and overwhelming. Please help me to face the coming days with courage and to rest in the assurance of Your presence and love. Watch over my sweet child. Amen.

Song
Newsboys. "Your Love Never Fails." *God's Not Dead.* InPop Records, 2011. CD.

Week 31 Day 2

"Shadrach, Meshach and Abednego replied to the king, "O Nebuchadnezzar, we do not need to defend ourselves before you in this matter. If we are thrown into the blazing furnace, the God we serve is able to save us from it, and he will rescue us from your hand, O king. But even if he does not, we want you to know, O king, that we will not serve your gods or worship the image of gold you have set up." (Dan. 3.16-19)

One of the hardest parts of faith involves surrendering your dreams and expectations so Christ can create something beyond your earthly imagination. As your Heavenly Father, God knows what's best for you and what will further His kingdom. So as you await your child's arrival, commit your life and that of your child's, to the Lord. Wait and see what the Lord has planned. For He is good, even when life doesn't seem to turn out the way you wanted. God is creating a masterpiece you will one day perceive and cherish.

Prayer

Dear Lord,

Help me to have an unwavering faith. Let my mouth declare the confidence I have in my heart during this pregnancy. May the new chapter of our lives be filled with Your love and a deeper understanding of Your grace. In Jesus' name, Amen.

Song

Third Day. "Trust in Jesus." *Move.* Essential Records, 2010. CD.

Week 31 Day 3

"The king's command was so urgent and the furnace so hot that the flames of the fire killed the soldiers who took up Shadrach, Meshach and Abednego, and these three men, firmly tied, fell into the blazing furnace. Then King Nebuchadnezzar leaped to his feet in amazement and asked his advisers, "Weren't there three men that we tied up and threw into the fire?...Then Nebuchadnezzar said, "Praise be to the God of Shadrach, Meshach and Abednego, who has sent his angel and rescued his servants! They trusted in him and defied the king's command and were willing to give up their lives rather than serve or worship any god except their own God. Therefore I decree that the people of any nation or language who say anything against the God of Shadrach, Meshach and Abednego be cut into pieces and their houses be turned into piles of rubble, for no other god can save in this way." (Dan. 3.22-29)

What an amazing testimony Shadrach, Meshach, and Abednego had. They held steadfast to their beliefs and God rewarded their faithfulness. Through their actions and commitment, God opened the eyes of an entire kingdom to the true God of Israel. After this miracle, King Nebuchadnezzar professed with his own tongue that, "...no other god can save in this way."

You may never fully comprehend the impact your words and actions have on those around you. Your life can be a light to the world that leads others to Christ. God is using you to show His love to the world, but first you must recognize the mercies He has bestowed upon you. Then you can lead others, like your child, to Christ.

Prayer

Dear Jesus,

Thank You for the amazing miracle of life inside of me. Help me to share my story with those around You. May they see the joy in my life and know that You are the Savior. May my child know You as her Savior all the days of her life. Amen.

Song

Kutless. "In Jesus' Name." *Glory.* BEC, 2014. CD.

Week 31 Day 4

"For by him all things were created: things in heaven and on earth, visible and invisible, whether thrones or powers or rulers or authorities; all things were created by him and for him. He is before all things, and in him all things hold together." (Col. 1.16-17)

The Almighty Creator of the universe has fashioned this child within you. With His powerful hands He has thoughtfully formed every part of your baby. He knew you would carry this child before the beginning of time, and soon you will hold God's masterpiece in your arms. When you are puzzled by God's design remember that "...in him all things hold together..." With His help, you will make a life with this child. He will guide you, comfort you, and strengthen you as you seek to glorify Him.

Prayer

Dear Lord,

I am humbled when I think of Your mighty hands making my child. Help me to always remember that it is with great love and tenderness that You brought this baby into being. You are my maker, and I know You have made me to glorify You. May our lives be a testimony of Your unfailing love. In Jesus' name, amen.

Song

August, Chris. "The Maker." *The Maker*. Fervent Records, 2015. CD.

Week 31 Day 5

"If you remain in me and my words remain in you, ask whatever you wish, and it will be given you." (John 15.7)

If you want to know God's will, immerse yourself in His word and prayer. Your fellowship with Christ will help you understand the teachings of Christ so that you will know how to pray. For even Jesus demonstrated how we should pray in the Garden of Gethsemane. In Matthew 26.39 Jesus says, "...My Father, if it is possible, may this cup be taken from me. Yet not as I will, but as you will." Even Jesus submitted to His Heavenly Father by surrendering His life. Christ accepted God's plan for Him because He loves His Heavenly Father and He loves you. He died on the cross to save you and to save your child. He wants you both to spend eternity with Him. Let Him hear your prayers.

Prayer
Dear Jesus,
Thank You for saving me and submitting to the agony of the cross in my place. Please reveal Your will and purpose through Your scripture and prayer. Let the fellowship of other believers guide me and encourage me in my faith life. Thank You for hearing my prayers.
Amen.

Song
Third Day. "Your Words." *Lead Us Back: Songs of Worship.* Essential Records, 2015. CD.

Week 32 Day 1

"When I am afraid I will trust in you." (Ps. 56.3)

This is a powerful verse that is worth committing to memory. In moments of desperation and apprehension, the Holy Spirit can use these words to fill you with confidence. Can you remember a time when God has delivered you from a dangerous or frightening situation? Those experiences serve to reaffirm your faith and to strengthen your resolve as you walk down the path God has provided. He has promised that no matter what lies ahead, He will be there.

"Trust in the Lord with all your heart and lean not on your own understanding; in all your ways acknowledge him, and he will make your paths straight." (Ps. 3.5-6)

Prayer

Lord,

Help me to trust in You when I am afraid. I know You are with me all the days of my life and in the midst of my fear. Please help me to rest in the promise of Your presence and Your care. Watch over my family and give me the courage I need to face the coming days with confidence and hope. In Jesus' name, amen.

Song

Jobe, Kari. "I Am Not Alone." *Majestic.* Sparrow Records, 2014. CD.

Week 32 Day 2

"Be my rock of refuge, to which I can always go; give the command to save me, for you are my rock and fortress…From birth, I have relied on you; you brought me forth from my mother's womb. I will ever praise you." (Ps. 71.3-6)

Praise the Lord for He is your "rock of refuge." God was there on the day of your birth, and He will be with you as you bring this child into the world. If this is your first delivery, then I would encourage you to remember your mother. She has a unique perspective on this pregnancy because it involves not only her grandchild, but also the child she brought into this world. She loves you and is probably very concerned about your safety, as well your child's. She knows the effort is takes to bring forth a child and to help a child grow. So be kind to the woman who helped raise you into the woman you are today and thank the Lord for the special person she is. Mothers can be a tremendous blessing throughout your life.

Prayer
Dear God,
You have always been there for me. I praise You for Your goodness and Your faithfulness. I ask You to be my fortress and my refuge as this incredible day comes closer. Please bless my child, and give me the courage to face this experience knowing You are with me always. Thank You for my mother and all that she has done throughout my life. In Jesus' name, amen.

Song
Bethel Music. "You Make Me Brave." *You Make Me Brave.* Bethel Music, 2014. CD.

Week 32 Day 3

"Be joyful in hope, patient in affliction, faithful in prayer."
(Rom. 12.12)

You're almost there! Write this verse on the tablet of your heart. When you are feeling impatient, remember these words and say a prayer. God will hear you. It wasn't until recently that the final part of this verse really resonated in my heart. It seems logical that if you are hopeful you will find joy and if you are patient during affliction you will be less frustrated, but "...faithful in prayer..." I know we should pray without ceasing, but how is prayer part of faithfulness? During the times I am dedicated to coming before the Lord in prayer, I have found myself better able to accomplish life's tasks and more prepared to face situations without feeling overwhelmed. So try it. Talk to your Savior and see how He blesses your faithfulness. Don't let life's distractions keep you from spending time in the presence of your Heavenly Father.

Prayer

Gracious Heavenly Father,

I am anxious to meet this child and I am tired of being uncomfortable. Please help me to be patient. Change my heart. Give me a heart that holds "...unswervingly to the hope we profess, for he who promised is faithful..."
(Heb. 10.23) Keep me close to You in prayer and guide my footsteps. In Jesus' name, amen.

Song

Hillsong United. "Touch the Sky." *Empires.* Hillsong, 2015. CD.

Week 32 Day 4

"When you lie down, you will not be afraid; when you lie down, your sleep will be sweet." (Prov. 3.24)

There were many nights I lay down to rest fearful of imminent, preterm labor. I would pray for God to watch over my children and help me through the long and uncomfortable hours of the night. In the morning, I would be overwhelmed with gratitude. For God had graciously allowed my children to grow safely for one more day. After saying a prayer of thanksgiving, I would again ask God to sustain me through the coming day. He was always faithful and available. No matter how many times I cried out in anguish, fear, sorrow, or exhaustion, God always heard my cry. May He grant you a restful night of sleep and refresh your spirit.

Prayer
Dear Jesus,
Thank You for the gift of sleep. Please grant me the rest I need to help this child grow and develop. Keep my heart steadfast in faith. In Jesus' name, amen.

Song
August, Chris. "Starry Night." *No Far Away*. Fervent Records, 2010. CD.

Week 32 Day 5

"Have I not commanded you? Be strong and courageous. Do not be terrified; do not be discouraged, for the Lord your God will be with you wherever you go." (Josh. 1.9)

Listen to the promise God has for you today. "The Lord your God will be with you wherever you go." Even in the valleys and uphill climbs of life, your Savior is walking with you. In the darkest moments, an outreached hand can provide indescribable comfort to someone facing an unknown future. As I rode in the back of an ambulance, I temporarily lost my vision due to a concussion. I couldn't see the first responder holding my hand, but I felt his grasp and it comforted me. In the middle of the darkness God reaches down in love and promises to never let go. With that knowledge you can "...be strong and courageous..." for the time is coming when you will have to face delivery with willingness and dedication. Your journey as a mother is about to begin and God will be holding you in the palm of His mighty hand.

Prayer
Lord,

Hold on to me as I approach the time of delivery. I know that labor is intense and painful, but I am reassured by Your promises. Please protect my child and give me the strength and ability to bring forth this new life. I yearn to cradle my child in my arms just as You embrace me. In Jesus' name, amen.

Song
Unspoken. "Start a Fire." *Unspoken.* Centricity Music, 2014. CD.

Week
33

Week 33 Day 1

"Find rest, O my soul in God alone; my hope comes from him. He alone is my rock and my salvation; he is my fortress, I will not be shaken." (Ps. 62.5)

In the last trimester, pregnancy can be very uncomfortable and tiring. It is easy to grow weary if you rely on your own strength. But God gives you hope because "...he is my fortress..." So as the days draw closer, find rest in God and joy in the future. As a Christian you are assured of your eternal salvation and the promise of a faithful God. Cling to Him and do not be shaken.

Prayer

Jesus,

Thank You for being my rock and my salvation. I have hope in the future because I know You are a loving and faithful God. Please give me the rest I need and help me when I do feel shaken. Watch over my precious baby as he continues to grow safely. Amen.

Song

Building 429. "We Won't Be Shaken." Essential Records, 2013. CD.

Week 33 Day 2

"But seek first his kingdom and his righteousness, and all these things will be given to you as well. Therefore do not worry about tomorrow, for tomorrow will worry about itself. Each day has enough trouble of its own." (Matt. 6.33-34)

As a mother it is easy to be consumed by worry, even when you know your Heavenly Father is watching over your family. God has made you a steward of many gifts, and He has called you to use your talents to serve Him. Therefore, it is good to remember that He is the Savior. You cannot control the universe, but you can bring your concerns, fears, and worries to the one who holds the universe in His hands, trusting that "…in all things God works for the good of those who love him, who have been called according to his purpose." (Rom. 8.28) As you endeavor to create a blessed home and a smooth delivery for your baby, recognize that is God holding you both within the palm of His hand every moment.

Prayer

Dear God,

Help me to seek You earnestly and to pursue Your word. Let me not be burdened or consumed with worry. Teach me to lay my fears at Your feet, so that I may walk in the confidence of Your loving mercy. In Jesus Name, Amen.

Song

Andrews, Meredith. "Not For a Moment." *Worth It All.* Word Worship, 2013. CD.

Week 33 Day 3

"And again, "I will put my trust in him." And again he says, "Here am I, and the children God has given me." Since the children have flesh and blood, he too shared in their humanity so that by his death he might destroy him who holds the power of death-that is the devil-and free those who all their lives were held in slavery by their fear of death. For surely it is not angels he helps, but Abraham's descendants. For this reason he had to be made like his brothers in every way, in order that he might become a merciful and faithful high priest in service to God, and that he might make atonement for the sins of the people." (Heb. 2.13-17)

Sometimes it is difficult for me to understand why God chose to send His only Son to die as atonement for my sins. For "...my thoughts are not your thoughts neither are your ways my ways..." declares the Lord." (Isa. 55.8) How could a holy and perfect God choose to become human and then offer Himself up as a blameless offering for my sin? He willingly gave up the glory of heaven to endure great suffering on our behalf. Now, He is our "...merciful and faithful high priest..." He continues to show us undeserved mercy and faithfulness. Therefore, "…I will put my trust in him..." He has proven His faithfulness countless times in the Bible. Think of your favorite stories and revisit them when you are discouraged. Remember the times God has rescued you and rejoice because Your Savior still reigns!

Prayer
Dear Merciful Heavenly Father,

Thank You for suffering in my place to redeem me. Teach me to surrender my will. Pour out Your Spirit in my heart and help me to follow where You lead. Forgive me for the times I attempt to force my will and help me to put my trust in You. In Jesus' Name, Amen.

Song
Mullins, Nicole. "My Redeemer Lives." *Nicole C. Mullen.* Word, 2000. CD.

Week 33 Day 4

"To you, O Lord, I lift up my soul; in you I trust, O my God."
(Ps. 25.1)

It's time to lift your hands up, woman of God! Cry out
to Jesus and lay your fears at His feet. Give God everything
that is in your heart and tell Him all that is in you. He knows
your needs before you even open your mouth. So give all
your worries to Jesus and sing His praises. When you
worship God, your soul is renewed and you are strengthened.
"My heart is steadfast, O God, my heart is steadfast I will sing
and make music." (Ps. 57.7)

Prayer
Dear Lord,
Hear the outpouring of my heart and restore my soul.
Take my life and make it Yours. May my heart ever praise
You and trust in Your unfailing love. Watch over my dear
child and guide me as I wait for the day when I will hold her
in my arms. In Jesus' name, amen.

Song
Camp, Jeremy."Take My Life." *Stay.* BEC, 2002. CD.

Week 33 Day 5

"Two are better than one, because they have a good return for their work: If one falls down, his friend can help him up." (Eccles. 4.9-10)

A beloved friend is more valuable than riches because together you can enjoy life's adventures. Fortunately, sorrows and trials can always be shared with a trusted companion, for "...a friend loves at all times..." (Prov. 17.17) If you find yourself without a female companion, don't be afraid to ask the giver of all good things to bestow a friend upon you. Ponder the love and compassion that has already been extended to you by fellow Christians during this phase of your life. For it is wonderful to see how God uses other people to bless our lives. As Christians we are called to help carry each other's burden, so let the women near you assist you, especially if you are on bed rest. Allowing them to show kindness to you enables them to experience the joy of giving as well. Then thank the Lord that you are dearly loved.

Prayer

Dear Jesus,

Thank You for the friends You have placed in my life. I pray You would help me to be the kind of friend I desire. Please fill my life with women who seek Your will and enjoy life. Help my child to be surrounded by friends and family who love her and You. Amen.

Song

Casting Crowns. "Just Be Held." *Thrive.* Reunion Records, 2014. CD.

Week
34

Week 34 Day 1

"I waited patiently for the Lord; he turned to me and heard my cry. He lifted me out of the slimy pit, out of the mud and mire; he set my feet on a rock and gave me a firm place to stand. He put a new song in my mouth, a hymn of praise to our God. Many will see and fear and put their trust in the Lord. Blessed is the man who makes the Lord his trust, who does not look to the proud, to those who turn aside to false gods. Many, O Lord my God, are the wonders you have done. The things you planned for us no one can recount to you; were I to speak and tell of them, they would be too many to declare." (Ps. 40.1-5)

Isn't it a beautiful feeling to know that you have the attention of the God of the universe? God is faithfully listening to all your prayers and praises. The world encourages you to trust in your own human capabilities, but in reality, only God's promises are steadfast. Therefore, trust in God and be assured that He has an incredible plan for you and your child. Remember the times God has provided for you and be uplifted because He is with you still.

Prayer
Dear Lord,
Thank you for hearing my cry and knowing the depths of my soul. Help me to trust in You to give me a firm place to stand. Forgive me when I am led astray by this world. I know You are my faithful provider. In Jesus' name, amen.

Song
Petra. "I Will Call Upon the Lord." *Petra Praise: Let the Rocks Cry Out*. Word, 1989. CD.

Week 34 Day 2

"Are not five sparrows sold for two pennies? Yet not one of them is forgotten by God. Indeed, the very hairs of your head are all numbered. Don't be afraid; you are worth more than many sparrows." (Luke 12.6-7)

What a beautiful illustration of your tender-hearted Creator. For many years I was comforted by the notion of being more important than a sparrow, but recently I have been more captivated by the intimate knowledge God has of me. Who else concerns himself with the hair are on your head? It is ever changing and yet, God is aware of the very essence of your being. He feels your inner turmoil, and He values you because you are made in His image. You are His own, precious child.

Prayer
Dearest Lord,

I am overwhelmed by the concern You have for me and the patience You show me. Thank You for loving me enough to listen and for answering my prayers. Please watch over my child. If it be your will, bring her into this world with all the strength and health a baby needs. Stand with me as we continue this journey down the road You have prepared. In Jesus' name, Amen.

Song
Big Daddy Weave. "Overwhelmed." *Love Come to Life.* Fervent Records, 2012. CD.

Week 34 Day 3

"Come to me, all you who are weary and burdened, and I will give you rest." (Matt. 11.28)

In the evenings, my heart and body would cry out for respite. "My soul finds rest in God alone; my salvation comes from him. He alone is my rock and my salvation; he is my fortress, I will never be shaken." (Ps. 62.12) If your mind is overwhelmed with tasks and worries, pray to Jesus because He will ease your burdens and strengthen your resolve to face tomorrow. He will calm your soul and restore you.

A woman asked me once what it felt like to carry twins. I told her it reminded me of when you're holding something very heavy for a long period of time and your muscles ache for you to let go. Only in a pregnancy, there is no relief for the weight you are carrying. That is why I believe God specifies in this verse "...weary and burdened..." It is one thing to be fatigued, but quite another to be weighed down from lifting. Worries are a tremendous burden. They overload you until you can no longer stand on your own. God beckons you to lay your troubles at the foot of His cross, and He will give you rest. He will carry the weight for you. "Do not let your hearts be troubled. Trust in God..." (John 14:1)

Prayer

Jesus,

I come before You in my weariness and need. This load I carry is too heavy for me. Please lift the weight of my sin and anxieties so that I may freely walk with You. Grant my heart and body the rest I need to shelter and grow this baby. I am eager for the day to come when I can hold my child in my arms. Please give me the patience and endurance I need as I await that day. Amen.

Song

Diaz, Jonny. "Just Breathe." *Everything Is Changing.* Centricity Music, 2015. CD.

Week 34 Day 4

"Taste and see that the Lord is good; blessed is the man who takes refuge in him." (Ps. 34.8)

During the 8th month your child sense of taste has developed, and she is aware of sounds outside of her body. (Lowdermilk, 344) She can recognize your voice and feel you moving. After she is born, she will be watching you every day and learning from your words and actions. Never underestimate the influence you will have on your child's spiritual life. With your guidance and by your example, you can instill in her that "...the Lord is good..." Teach her to take refuge in Him just as you have. Tell her how the Lord has delivered you in your life and sustained you in this pregnancy.

"We may not be able to prepare the future for our children, but we can at least prepare our children for the future."
–Franklin D. Roosevelt

Prayer
Dear Jesus,
You are good! I will praise Your holy name. Thank You for being my refuge and my strength. Forgive me when I fail to understand Your ways and when I forget that in all things You work for the good of those who love You. Amen.

Song
Plumb, "Great Is Our God." *Exhale.* Curb. 2015. CD.

Week 34 Day 5

"The Lord is righteous in all his ways and loving toward all he has made. The Lord is near to all who call on him, to all who call on him in truth. He fulfills the desires of those who fear him; he hears their cry and saves them. The Lord watches over all who love him, but the wicked he will destroy." (Ps. 145.17-20)

One Saturday a pair of runaway poodles came running into our backyard and frightened our 9-month old cat, Sherbert, up a tree. She stayed in that tree all night mewing and crying. Every attempt to retrieve her from the pine tree only made her crawl towards the top. Finally, unable to help, we left her alone in the cold and rain. In the morning, my children watched in horror as she fell out of the tree! Sherbert looked miserable with her frozen, wet fur and terrified eyes, but she was alive. We had all prayed for her safe descent and God granted it! I was amazed by God's faithfulness and concern for even the smallest of creatures.

How often do we run away from safety and towards danger? When we fail to seek God's guidance, we step out onto perilous branches alone. It's cold and lonely when we turn away from God, but He waits patiently for our return; ready to catch us in His strong, loving arms.

Prayer

Dear Jesus, My Savior,

I know You care about all You have made, including my baby. I pray You will deliver us safely through this pregnancy. Watch over my baby and keep him safe. Amen.

Song

Mandisa. "He is With You." *Freedom.* Sparrow. 2009. CD.

Week 35 Day 1

"Reckless words pierce like a sword, but the tongue of the wise brings healing." (Ps. 12.18)

I have a dear friend who often says, "I'm going to receive that." Or, "I'm not going to receive that." At first I chuckled at her words, but as I began to understand what she meant, I realized it was quite profound. We can allow someone to speak life over us and refuse to let them speak "death," or spiritual harm, regarding our circumstances. It is necessary to disregard and sometimes refute those who would cause you to lose faith, or who are reckless with their words. You will feel empowered when you choose to respond to negative comments with, "I'm not going to receive that." You may hear their words, but you will not accept them or give them power over your life. God knows your needs, and He will provide for you. Seek the Lord, for the Lord gives wisdom and from His mouth come knowledge and understanding.

Prayer

Lord,

You know all things. Give me the wisdom I need to discern between the truth of God and the lies of this world. Surround me with people who will lift me up in prayer and with their words. Help me to speak kindly to those around me and to remember that we are all Your imperfect children in need of forgiveness. Bless my child. In Jesus' name, Amen.

Song

TobyMac. "Speak Life." *Eye On It.* Forefront Records, 2012. CD.

Week 35 Day 2

"Unless the Lord builds the house, its builders labor in vain. Unless the Lord watches over the city, the watchmen stand guard in vain. In vain you rise early and stay up late, toiling for food to eat-for he grants sleep to those he loves."
(Ps. 127.1-2)

At 35 weeks, your child is about 5 1/2 pounds and has formed sleeping patterns. There is fat under his skin that makes it appear less wrinkly. You will also be delighted to know his muscles and bones are now completely developed. (U.S. National Library of Medicine, Web)

You are probably already keenly aware of the incredible blessing sleep can be for you and your baby. You may choose to work incessantly to accomplish temporal tasks, but ultimately you will have to acknowledge that all good things come from above and are not entirely a result of your efforts. Work is necessary, but it is good to rest in the Lord's provision, especially before and after the birth a child. He will know that you love her even when chores are left undone.

"The success of love is in the loving-it is not in the result of loving. Of course it is natural in love to want the best for the other person, but whether it turns out that way or not does not determine the value of what we have done."
–Mother Teresa

Prayer

Lord,

Please help my family to serve You and to place You first in our lives. Forgive me when I try to control every aspect of my life to ensure a successful future. Help us to rest securely in Your love and faithfulness. Watch over my dear child as the day is upon us. Bring my baby into this world at the time You have ordained and with Your blessing.

In Jesus' name, Amen.

Song

Casting Crowns. "Life of Praise." *Casting Crowns.* Reunion Records, 2003. CD.

Week 35 Day 3

"The Lord gives strength to his people; the Lord blesses his people with peace." (Ps. 29.11)

Your Heavenly Father is the best gift-giver! He always knows just what you need and He generously blesses those who love Him. Who else can bring peace or rejuvenation in the midst of difficult circumstances and long days? If you are feeling downhearted, try and count your blessings. You may be greatly encouraged by the bountiful gifts God has bestowed upon you and your family. This miracle growing inside of you is evidence of the Heavenly Father's love.

Prayer

Dear Father,

Your blessings overwhelm me. Your mercy endures forever! Thank You for granting me peace when I am anxious and strength when I am weak. Take care of my baby and help him grow according to Your will. May Your love surround us as we await his arrival. In Jesus' name, amen.

Song

Peters, Moriah. "You Carry Me." *Brave.* Essential Records, 2014. CD.

Week 35 Day 4

"Then I thought, 'To this I will appeal; the years when the Most High stretched out his right hand. I will remember the deeds of the Lord; yes, I will remember your miracles of long ago.'" (Ps. 77.10-11)

When I reflect on my past and look for evidence of God's mighty hand, I am most often reminded of events concerning my family. Once when my sons were just a few years old, they climbed upon their dresser to watch their daddy drive the tractor in the side yard. As I entered their room, I was shocked to see them both leaning onto the screen of their large, upstairs window. Three sides of the screen had been pushed out by their weight as they peered fearlessly out of the window. How had they not gone completely through the window? I still believe it took an angel's hand to keep my sons from falling to the ground below. Initially, I was horrified and stricken with guilt. Yet eventually, I was overcome with thankfulness and relief because I realized that we were not raising them alone. God is with us as we seek to bring up our children in the way of the Lord. Our Heavenly Father chooses to use imperfect people, like you and me, to accomplish His perfect will. He has given you this child and the opportunity to share the good news with your family. So remember the deeds the Lord has done in your life and tell them to your children.

Prayer

Almighty God,

Thank You for remembering me and for helping me in every situation. I am amazed every time I feel Your presence and remember the goodness You have shown me. Forgive me when I fail to recognize Your hand and help me to speak of Your love to those dearest to me. May my life be a living testimony of Your great love. In Jesus' name, amen.

Song

Tomlin, Chris. "Good Good Father." *Good Good Father.* Six Steps Records, 2015. CD.

Week 35 Day 5

"Delight yourself in the Lord and he will give you the desires of your heart." (Ps. 37.4)

When I was in 8th grade, my pastor chose this verse as my confirmation verse. Over the years, I have come to realize that this verse encapsulates my life. I thought happiness would be found in the fulfillment of specific goals, but God has graciously shown me time and again that true joy is found in walking with your Savior.

Can you think of a time when God has turned your crooked paths into something wonderful? Ponder the times when God has revealed His majesty to you with amazing and unexpected opportunities. As you treasure those memories, you will be reassured of His great care for you and the child that will soon change your life. This baby will bring you joy and heartache, laughter, and tears. Your heart will swell with a deep and permeating love for the beautiful gift God has bestowed upon you. So rejoice! God wants to fulfill your deepest longings with His gracious love.

Prayer
Dear God,

I commit my way to You and I ask You to free me from my anxiety. I lay my fears and uncertainties at the foot of Your cross. Help me to trust that Your help will come at the right time. In Jesus' name, amen.

Song
Battistelli, Francesca. "Write Your Story." *If We're Honest.* Fervent Records, 2014. CD.

Week

36

Week 36 Day 1

"My soul is in anguish. How long, O Lord, how long? Turn, O Lord, and deliver me; save me because of your unfailing love...I am worn out from groaning; all night long I flood my bed with weeping and drench my couch with tears. My eyes grow weak with sorrow...The Lord has heard my cry for mercy; the Lord accepts my prayer." (Ps. 6.3-9)

You are so close to bringing your precious child into this world! God hears your pleas for mercy and feels the anguish of your body and soul. He knows the hour and the day you eagerly await. Take heart, for He is with you as the arrival of your little one approaches. God has designed your body to protect, nourish, and develop your sweet baby completely. It is in His infinite wisdom that He made the days of pregnancy last 40 weeks. Right now, your child is becoming physically able to thrive outside of your womb. Do not underestimate the praiseworthy undertaking you are performing with every passing day. Soon, you will see your reward.

"As mothers, we are building great cathedrals. We cannot be seen if we're doing it right. And one day, it is very possible that the world will marvel, not only at what we built, but at the beauty that has been added to the world by the sacrifices of invisible women."
-Nicole Johnson

Prayer

Dear Jesus,

My heart and body ache. I beg You to continue to give me strength and patience. Help me to wait these final days out with renewed hope because of Your love. Wrap Your arms around my child and me, for we are in Your hands. Amen.

Song

Tomlin, Chris. "Whom Shall I Fear." *Burning Lights.* Six Step Records, 2013. CD.

Week 36 Day 2

"I will exalt you, my God the King; I will praise your name forever and ever. Every day I will praise you and extol your name for ever and ever." (Ps.145.1-2)

I heard it said once that if you clear a child's playroom of all the clutter, she will inevitably begin to dance. Her heart will delight in the open space as she spins in gleeful circles across the floor. Out of curiosity, I tried it, and it worked! My children loved having an open area in which to play.

Can you clear your mind of all your responsibilities and stresses to focus on Jesus? When you take time every day to present your requests to the Lord and to praise Him, you will find joy. God wants you to be happy and He loves to hear you pray. Let Him see you dance across the floor of creation with a song of praise in your heart.

Prayer
Dear Lord,

I praise You and exalt You as my God and King. Fill my heart with gladness. May my life be a celebration of all You have done for me. You are wonderful and worthy of all my praise! In Jesus' name, amen.

Song
Chapman, Steven. "Lord of the Dance." *Signs of Life*. Sparrow. 1996. CD.

Week 36 Day 3

"I consider that our present sufferings are not worth comparing with the glory that will be revealed in us. The creation waits in eager expectation for the sons of God to be revealed. For the creation was subjected to frustration, not by its own choice, but by the will of the one who subjected it, in hope that the creation itself will be liberated from its bondage to decay and brought into the glorious freedom of the children of God. We know that the whole creation has been groaning as in the pains of childbirth right up to the present time. Not only so, but we ourselves, who have the firstfruits of the Spirit, groan inwardly as we wait eagerly for our adoption as sons, the redemption of our bodies. For in this hope we were saved. But hope that is seen is no hope at all. Who hopes for what he already has? But if we hope for what we do not yet have, we wait for it patiently." (Rom. 8.18-25)

Your faith in Jesus gives you hope because you know your eternal destiny. As God's child, you can look forward to the day of Christ's return, just as you eagerly anticipate the birth of this child. You hope for a happy, healthy child even though you cannot see her tiny hands and feet yet. You do not have to see her to believe she is there because you can feel her movements and see your body changing. I pray that your heart is at peace concerning the welfare of your child and that fear has no foothold in your life. May the Lord reassure you with His presence in every circumstance throughout this pregnancy. When you face difficulties in this world, remember that this is not our home. We wait for Christ's return when all will be made new.

Prayer

Dear Jesus,

I know my present condition is temporary, but I beseech You to comfort me with Your gentle hand and soothe my anxious heart. Help me to look forward to the coming days with hope. Thank You for bringing us through this pregnancy. I know You are faithful and You promise to always be with me. As the days draw near for my delivery, please prepare my heart and my body to bring this child into the world safely. Let Your will be done. Amen.

Song

Building 429. "Where I Belong." *Listen to the Sound.* Essential Records, 2011. CD.

Week 36 Day 4

"Great is the Lord and most worthy of praise; his greatness no one can fathom. The generation will commend your works to another; they will tell of your mighty acts. They will speak of the glorious splendor of your majesty, and I will meditate on your works. They will tell of the power of your awesome works, and I will proclaim your great deeds." (Ps. 145.3-6)

You can see evidence of the Holy Spirit in the hearts of baptized believers and the actions of those motivated by the power of the Holy Spirit. Soon, you will also see proof of God's amazing handiwork in the birth of your child. As you cradle your tiny miracle of life in your arms, you will be astonished by the intricate fingers and toes on your baby. When your heart is filled to overflowing, may your mouth proclaim His wonderful works. As your child grows, instill in him the greatness of His creator. Praise the Lord for your time is coming soon!

Prayer
Dearest Jesus,

My heart is filled with joyful anticipation as the birth of my child approaches. I praise You for your kindness and the splendor of Your works. May my heart and mouth tell the world of Your great deeds! In Jesus's name, Amen.

Song
Grace, Jamie. "Beautiful Day." *Ready To Fly.* Gotee Records, 2014. CD.

Week 36 Day 5

"Your kingdom is an everlasting kingdom, and your dominion endures through all generations. The Lord is faithful to all his promises and loving toward all he has made. The Lord upholds all those who fall and lifts up all who are bowed down. The eyes of all look to you, and you give them their food at the proper time. You open your hand and satisfy the desires of every living thing." (Ps. 145.13-15)

God fulfills our insufficiencies and desires with what we need at the appropriate time. Imagine the chaos and pain that would ensue if God gave us everything we desired when we requested it. It would be comparable to giving a toddler only the candy he demanded, rather than providing him with healthy food to nourish his growing body. Initially, the child would be appeased, but eventually he would become unhealthy and miserable. In the same way, God is mindful of your well-being and your needs. He will give you the desires of your heart at the proper time. Your baby will come in God's timing, and He will provide for you both out of His rich mercy and love.

Prayer

Dear Lord,

Please help me to trust in Your timing and your willingness to provide for all our needs. I long to have the desires of my heart filled immediately, but I know You are working in my life for my good. Please protect my child and me. In Jesus' name, amen.

Song

Shust, Aaron. "My Savior My God." *Anything Worth Saying.* Brash Records, 2005. CD.

Week

37

Week 37 Day 1

"Then he said to them, "My soul is overwhelmed with sorrow to the point of death. Stay here and keep watch with me." Going a little farther, he fell with his face to the ground and prayed, "My Father, if it is possible, may this cup be taken from me. Yet not as I will, but as you will." (Matt. 26.38-39)

During my first pregnancy I remember crying in my husband's arms and saying, "I changed my mind. I'm tired of being sick!" I was very foolish with my words because I was overcome with self-pity. I could not comprehend the blessing my daughter would be in our lives or how worthwhile my discomfort was. Thankfully, Jesus is not irresolute or careless in His speaking. As you contemplate this passage of Jesus in Gethsemane, you can be reassured that Christ knows what it's like to be overwhelmed. He understands your suffering and He demonstrates how prayer helps you remain steadfast in the midst of difficult times. Jesus asked His Father if there was another way, but ultimately He took the punishment for our sin and died because He loves us. He cares for you far more than you adore your unborn child. Therefore, cry out to the one who knows your needs and provides for you.

Prayer
Dear God,
Draw me close to You as the day of my child's birth draws near. Help me to trust in You and surrender to Your will. Take care of my precious baby. In Jesus' name, amen.

Song
King and Country. "Fix My Eyes." *Fix My Eyes.* Fervent Records, 2014. CD.

Week 37 Day 2

"A bruised reed he will not break, and a smoldering wick he will not snuff out, till he leads justice to victory. In his name the nations will put that hope." (Matt.12.20-21)

When you find yourself beaten down by the weight of your condition or circumstances, cry out to God for mercy and let Him encourage you through His words above. Even during times of great suffering God is steadfast. He is waiting for you to call out to Him to uplift and guide you. Remember that nothing can snatch you or your child from your Heavenly Father's mighty hand. Put your hope in His faithfulness and His promise of salvation as your day of delivery draws closer.

Prayer
Dear Jesus,
I feel like I'm barely holding on. I am tired and worn out. You have promised to keep me from breaking and I beseech You to uphold me in these final days of preparation. Help me to look to You for peace, comfort, and strength. Watch over my baby as the day of arrival draws near. Amen.

Song
Shust, Aaron. "My Hope Is In You." *Fix My Eyes.* Fervent Records, 2014. CD.

Week 37 Day 3

"There is a time for everything, and a season for every activity under heaven: a time to be born...He has made everything beautiful in its time. He has also set eternity in the hearts of men; yet they cannot fathom what God has done from beginning to end." (Eccles. 3:1-11)

Cherish the time you are pregnant with your child because God has bestowed upon you a tremendous blessing. You are a mother! Only you can feel this miracle growing and moving inside your womb. Therefore, this is a season to treasure because it will not last long. Right now, within your womb, your child is growing in the safest and most beneficial environment designed by God. Every day of this season is a gift. It won't be long before you hold your child and see the face that you so long to love. As for now, enjoy the experience that God has given only to you!

Prayer
Dear God
Thank You for the miracle growing inside of me. Help me to cherish the time that I am carrying my baby. I am grateful for this wonderful gift You have given me, and I praise You for the things I have yet to see and experience. In Jesus' name, Amen.

Song
Chapman, Steven. "Something Beautiful." *Glorious Unfolding.* Reunion Records, 2013. CD.

Week 37 Day 4

"For this reason, since the day we heard about you, we have not stopped praying for you and asking God to fill you with the knowledge of his will through all spiritual wisdom and understanding...being strengthened with all power according to his glorious might so that you may have great endurance and patience, and joyfully giving thanks to the Father, who has qualified you to share in the inheritance of the saints in the kingdom of light." (Col. 1.9-12)

The first time a friend prayed over me I was deeply touched by her sincere concern. Her boldness in openly presenting our requests to God together still inspires me. Prayer is a powerful tool and a merciful privilege. God longs to listen to your prayers and petitions because He is compassionate. Do you have the courage to share your heart and mind with your Heavenly Father? God can transform a heart through the gift of prayer and the Holy Spirit. He invites you to come to Him and find peace and joy in His wisdom and strength.

"I have been driven many times to my knees by the overwhelming conviction that I had nowhere else to go." -Abraham Lincoln

Prayer

Dear Jesus,

Help me to share my heart with You. Grant me the peace only You can give and lead me in Your ways. Amen.

Song

7eventh Time Down. "Just Say Jesus." *Just Say Jesus.* BEC Recordings, 2013. CD.

Week 37 Day 5

"Blessed is the man who perseveres under trial, because when he has stood the test, he will receive the crown of life that God has promised those who love him." (Jas. 1.12)

Are you afraid of labor and delivery? You alone have been given the task of carrying this child and bringing him into the world. God does not give us a spirit of fear, but encourages us in Isaiah to "...Be strong, do not fear; your God will come..." (Isa. 35.4) God will be with you. Pray for the medical staff that will be assisting in your delivery and for your husband and child. Cover yourselves in prayer and lay your concerns at Jesus' feet because He cares for you. The God who has promised you the crown of eternal life will help you persevere.

Prayer
Dear God,
Please give me courage and strength to deliver this dear child. Give the medical staff wisdom and the ability to provide the care we need. Help my husband and family to support me with love and affirmation. Help me to persevere in this trial and to press on toward the goal of eternal life. In Jesus' name, amen.

Song
Mandisa."Overcomer." *Overcomer*. Sparrow, 2013. CD.

Week
38

Week 38 Day 1

"Blessed are those whose strength is in you, who have set their hearts on pilgrimage." (Ps. 84.5)

This is it. You are almost there! The day of your delivery is upon you, and you have set your heart on it. Now is the time to remember where your strength comes from. Prepare your heart and mind by focusing on Christ's guiding light. May God bless you and your child. May He give you strength, courage, and peace. Let the words from the scriptures assure you of His presence and His great love. I pray the Holy Spirit will give you faith in your Savior until He takes you both home. Praise the Lord and may He keep your heard steadfast!

Prayer

Dear Lord,

Thank You for bringing me this far on my pilgrimage. Please sustain me with Your strength and grant me confidence in Your faithfulness. Prepare my heart and mind for this experience. Help me to cling to Your promises.

In Jesus' name, Amen.

Song

Rend Collective. "My Lighthouse." *The Flood*. Integrity Music, 2013. CD.

Week 38 Day 2

"Lift your eyes and look to the heavens; Who created all these? He who brings out the starry host one by one, and calls them each by name. Because of his great power and mighty strength, not one of them is missing. Why do you say, O Jacob, and complain, O Israel, "My way is hidden from the Lord; my cause is disregarded by my God"? Do you not know? Have you not heard? The Lord is the everlasting God, the Creator of the ends of the earth. He will not grow tired or weary, and his understanding no one can fathom. He gives strength to the weary and increases the power of the weak. Even youths grow tired and weary, and young men stumble and fall; but those who hope in the Lord will renew their strength. They will soar on wings like eagles; they will run and not grow weary, they will walk and not be faint."
(Isa. 40.26-31)

Towards the end of my pregnancy, I remember getting chastised by a dental hygienist for my poor dental care. I was embarrassed and somewhat angry because this young woman could not comprehend how incredibly exhausted I was. Sometimes, just brushing my teeth was an overwhelming task. God, however, understands our limited supply of energy because Jesus walked on this earth as a man. Consequently, He knowingly offers a wonderful gift for women who are weak, frightened, and uncomfortable, "…he gives strength to the weary…" I beseech you to ask for His help and then receive the power only God can bestow. Trust in His ability to deliver and restore you, for that is how great His concern is for you. He is willing and able to sustain you with all that you need.

Prayer

Dear Heavenly Father,

I am weary and burdened. Please uphold me through this difficult time and reassure me with Your presence and love. Fill me with Your spirit so that I may ever praise You. In Jesus Name, Amen.

Song

Camp, Jeremy. "Everlasting God." *We Cry Out: The Worship Project.* BEC, 2010. CD.

Week 38 Day 3

"You may ask me for anything in my name, and I will do it."
(John 14.14)

What an incredible promise Jesus makes in this verse! One may be tempted to start envisioning God as a genie in a bottle who grants our every wish. However, I don't believe that's what Jesus intended. It is apparent that He wants us to present our requests to God, but in a manner that recognizes His divine sovereignty. He does not tell us to ask in our own name or even our loved one's name. Jesus says, "ask me for anything in my name, and I will do it." It's not a matter of our persistence or desperation, but rather if it furthers the kingdom of God. I do firmly believe God can be persuaded by our pleas, but God has a divine plan. He loves you, and in His wisdom He wants to bless you. His ways are higher than our ways. Just as you will know what is best for your child at 2 years old, no matter how many times he asks, whines, demands, or cries to get his way. You will do what is best for him because you love him. God loves you with a perfect love that is even greater than yours for your child.

Prayer
Dear Jesus,

Help me to pray according to Your will and to find peace in the certainty of Your great love for me. Please be merciful to me and hear my pleas. Give my heart the faith I need to trust in You. Amen.

Song
Big Daddy Wave. "The Only Name." *Love Came To Life.* Fervent Records, 2012. CD.

Week 38 Day 4

"God is our refuge and strength, an ever-present help in trouble. Therefore we will not fear, though the earth give way and the mountains fall into the heart of the sea, though its waters roar and foam and the mountains quake with their surging." (Ps. 46.1-2)

Labor is intense and overwhelming, but you have a God whom you trust. You can have fearless confidence because you know the same God who formed the mountains can stop the seas from surging with just the sound of His voice. Therefore, do not fear because your Almighty God is with you. He has promised to remain steadfast throughout your storms until the waters are calm.

Prayer
Dear Lord,
Please be near me during my labor and delivery. Give me the confidence and strength I need. Help me to remember amidst my suffering that my pain will pass. I know I will meet my precious child in just a short time. So hold my child close to Your heart and safely in Your hands until that day. In Jesus' name, Amen.

Song
Jesus Culture. "One Thing Remains." *Come Away*. Sparrow Records, 2015. CD.

Week 38 Day 5

The Healing of a Boy With a Demon

"When they came to the crowd, a man approached Jesus and knelt before him. Lord, but have mercy on my son," he said. "He has seizures and is suffering greatly. He often falls into the fire or into the water. I brought him to your disciples, but they could not heal him."

"O unbelieving and perverse generation," Jesus replied, "how long shall I stay with you? How long shall I put up with you? Bring the boy here to me." Jesus rebuked the demon, and it came out of the boy, and he was healed from that moment. Then the disciples came to Jesus in private and asked, "Why couldn't we drive it out?" He replied, "Because you have so little faith. I tell you the truth, if you have faith as small as a mustard seed, you can say to this mountain, 'Move from here to there' and it will move. Nothing will be impossible for you." (Matt. 17.14-20)

This passage reveals Jesus' great compassion for those who are suffering and for parents with sick children. Jesus rebuked the demon that tormented the boy the moment his father came to Him and begged for mercy. Jesus does not want us to be tortured by Satan or his demons. He came to save us from death and sin's destruction. When in faith, the father brought his problems directly to the Savior, Jesus showed immense mercy.

Jesus still reigns! The power of a living and active faith is emphasized by Jesus' insistence that "...nothing will be impossible for you..." if you have faith as small as a mustard seed. Often times, people believe that our ability to change a situation is based on how big or strong our faith is, but that isn't what Jesus says. God can work miracles, like moving mountains, through faith as small as a tiny mustard seed. If it brings about God's plan to further His kingdom, it will be done. His ability to accomplish great things is not inhibited by our spiritual limitations. So lay your requests before the Savior of the world. For He shows mercy and compassion to all His children.

Prayer
Dear Jesus,
     I ask you to .... If it is your will Lord, move this mountain! Let this obstacle be removed if it brings You glory. If it does not, then give me peace while I am waiting and the gift of faith when You lovingly tell me, "No." In Jesus' name, Amen.

Song
Daigle, Lauren. "Trust in You" *How Can It Be.* Centricity Music, 2014. CD.

Week 39 Day 1

"He who dwells in the shelter of the Most High will rest in the shadow of the Almighty. I will say of the Lord, `He is my refuge and my fortress, my God, in whom I trust.'" (Ps. 91.1-2)

Have you ever traveled abroad? As soon as the plane touches the ground in the United States, I feel relieved because I know I am secure within our borders. It is exciting to see the rest of the world, but I am grateful for my homeland and the protection it provides. You have an even better shelter in this world, for as a believer in Jesus Christ, you are a citizen of the Kingdom of God. All who dwell "...in the shelter of the Most High will rest in the shadow of the Almighty..." Just as a young child cling's to the leg of his parent in unfamiliar situations, may you always hold tightly to your Heavenly Father. You are a privileged, guarded, and treasured child of God. So trust in your Omnipotent Savior, for He is your refuge.

Prayer

Almighty God,

Thank You for inviting me into Your kingdom. May my family and I ever dwell in Your presence. I thank You for the gift of safety and protection. Watch over my sweet baby as I await the day of her arrival. In Jesus' name, amen.

Song

Gray, Jason. "Good to be Alive." *A Way to See In the Dark.* Centricity Music, 2011. CD.

Week 39 Day 2

"But now listen, O Jacob, my servant, Israel, whom I have chosen. This is what the Lord says-he who made you, who formed you in the womb, and who will help you: Do not be afraid, O Jacob, my servant, Jeshurun, whom I have chosen. For I will pour water on the thirsty land, and streams on the dry ground; I will pour out my Spirit on your offspring, and my blessing on your descendants. They will spring up like grass in a meadow, like poplar trees by flowing. One will say, 'I belong to the Lord'; another will call himself by the name of Jacob; still another will write on his hand, 'The Lord's' and will take the name Israel. (Isa. 44)

Your legacy is growing within you and will be arriving soon. One of your greatest responsibilities will involve raising this child to know his Savior. In turn, your faith will be passed down for generations. What a beautiful inheritance you will leave! God has chosen you specifically for this task and He has tenderly created you for this purpose. The Holy Spirit will equip and empower you. Therefore, when you are uncertain, call on the God who calls you by your name. He will help you.

Prayer
Dear Heavenly Father,
Help me as I seek to raise up my child in the knowledge of You. Fill me with Your Holy Spirit so that I will be prepared for the work You have given me, Jesus. Amen.

Song
We Are the Messengers. "Everything Comes Alive." *Everything Comes Alive.* Word Records, 2015. CD.

Week 39 Day 3

"Her children arise and call her blessed; her husband also, and he praises her: Many women do noble things, but you surpass them all." Charm is deceptive, and beauty is fleeting; but a woman who fears the Lord is to be praised." (Prov. 31.29-30)

If you are seeking accolades and recognition you will not find them in motherhood. However, you will discover moments of great joy. With your child's first smile; your son's bouquet of dandelions; an invitation to a kitchen set feast; you will realize the greatest rewards are presented by your children. My Mom once told me that out of all her accomplishments she was proudest of her children. What an inspiration! Even our Savior's mother, Mary, "…treasured up all these things and pondered them in her heart." (Luke 2.19) Delight in the happiness your children will bring and the blessings God has given you.

A rose can say "I love you,"
orchids can enthrall,
but a weed bouquet in a chubby fist,
yes, that says it all.
-Anonymous

Prayer
Dear Jesus,
Thank You for the gift of children and their precious love. Help me to teach them of Your perfect love. Amen.

Song
Chapman, Steven. "One Heartbeat at a Time. "*This Moment. Sparrow, 2015. CD.*

Week 39 Day 4

"What other nation is so great as to have their gods near them the way the Lord our God is near us whenever we pray to him?" (Deut. 4.7)

As you endure the final days of this pregnancy, may your heart be steadfast through faith in your Everlasting God. Share the emotions overflowing within you with your Heavenly Father so that He may give you the courage you need to bravely face labor and delivery. He knows how dedicated you have been to growing this beautiful baby in the past several months because He has suffered alongside you. Now it is time to trust in Him to help you bring this wonderful blessing into this world.

Prayer

My Dearest Savior,

Thank You for being so near me when I pray. Please calm my soul and help me to remember that You are with me in these final days of pregnancy. You know when my baby will come, and I trust You to help me bring him into this world. Thank You for the blessing of Your presence and I pray You will give me boldness of spirit to face delivery. Amen.

Song

Big Daddy Weave. "Hold Me Jesus." *Every Time I Breathe.* Fervent Records, 2006. CD.

Week 39 Day 5

"When Jesus saw his mother there, and the disciple whom he loved standing nearby, he said to his mother, "Dear woman, here is your son," and to the disciple, "Here is your mother." From that time on, this disciple took her into his home." (John 19. 26-27)

In His final moments on the cross, Jesus remembered His mother. Out of His great mercy and love, He provided for the woman who delivered Him into this world. Jesus asked the disciple He loved to take care of His mother, Mary. Isn't that a beautiful detail in the story of Calvary? Even in the midst of His suffering, Jesus was mindful of His mother. Now, during one of your greatest trials, God is with you. He knows your needs and He will provide for you also, dear mother-to-be. May you rest in His merciful care and trust in His promise to be with you.

Prayer
Dear Jesus,

Thank You for remembering my child and me. Hold us forever in Your hand. Give my heart peace as I await the coming of my child. Thank You for showing mercy and love to us. Amen.

Song
Story, Laura. "Mighty to Save." *Great God Who Saves*. Fair Trade Services, 2008. CD.

Week

40

Week 40 Day 1

"You will keep in perfect peace him whose mind is steadfast, because he trusts in you. Trust in the Lord forever, for the Lord, the Lord, is the Rock eternal." (Isa. 26.3-4)

The time is upon you! The wonderful treasure you have been seeking is soon to be revealed. Do not let the fear of delivery rob you of this joyful time. Keep your mind steadfast by meditating on your favorite passages, listening to Christian music, and conversing with your Heavenly Father. Congratulations on making it to week 40!

Prayer
Dearest Jesus,
Be my rock, Lord! Keep my mind and heart firm and devoted. I am excited to meet my child and to hold the one I carry every day. Fill me with Your peace and help me to trust in Your faithfulness. Amen.

Song
Gray, Jason. "Remind Me Who I Am." *A Way to See in the Dark.* Centricity Music, 2011. CD.

Week 40 Day 2

"When I am afraid, I will trust in you. In God, whose word I praise, in God I trust; I will not be afraid. What can mortal man do to me?" (Ps. 56.3-4)

It is normal to be fearful of delivery, but you have a God that is faithful in all circumstances. You are not alone. God has raised up people to provide the care you need. Trust in the Lord to guide the hands of the medical staff as they help you bring your baby into the world. Pray for those who will participate in your child's delivery, and may God bless your coming endeavor.

Prayer
Dear Jesus,

Bind this verse on the tablet of my heart. Help me to trust in You. Let fear have no power over me because You are in control. If it be Your will, bring my child into this world safely and without problems. In all things, let remember Your goodness. Amen.

Song
Crowder, "I Am." *Neon Steeple.* Six Steps Records, 2014. CD.

Week 40 Day 3

"We wait in hope for the Lord; he is our help and our shield. In him our hearts rejoice, for we trust in his holy name. May your unfailing love rest upon us, O Lord, even as we put our hope in you." (Ps. 33.20-22)

Labor is a battle. The intensity of the contractions necessary to bring forth this new life is harrowing. Yet, you are not defenseless! God is described as your shield. He will not let leave you alone to face this challenge. It says His faithful love will "...rest upon..." you. Like a shield and a blanket of comfort, God will stand with you to the end. Remember this is a battle, not a war. This brief moment in time is difficult, but it is only a fraction of the amazing journey God has planned for you.

Prayer
God,

Help me in this battle. Let me not be overcome with fear, but hope. Cover me with Your presence and protect both my child and me during delivery. I need You, Lord. Please be with us. In Jesus' name, amen.

Song
Plumb. "In My Arms." *Blink.* Curb Records, 2007. CD.

Week 40 Day 4

"A woman giving birth to a child has pain because her time has come; but when her baby is born she forgets the anguish because of her joy that a child is born into the world." (John 16.21)

If you are frightened of labor and delivery, take heart, for God has claimed you as His own. He exclaims, "So do not fear, for I am with you; do not be dismayed, for I am your God. I will strengthen you and help you; I will uphold you with my righteous right hand." (Isa. 41.10)

Remember, people choose to have additional children because they have learned that the happiness children bring to life surpasses every temporary pain and struggle you are enduring now. Rejoice! Soon you will meet your beautiful baby.

Prayer

Lord,

I am afraid, but I am placing my hope in You. Help me to look through the eyes of eternity and know that labor is a short moment in time. Give me strength and courage to bring forth the baby You have created to be part of our family. Watch over us and bless this delivery. Please help the medical staff who will assist us by granting them wisdom and skill. Please protect my child and help me to remember that we are always within Your grasp. In Jesus' name, amen.

Song

Building 429. "We Won't Be Shaken." *We Won't Be Shaken.* Praise Hymn, 2013. CD.

Week 40 Day 5

"Jesus said, `Let the little children come to me, and do not hinder them, for the kingdom of heaven belongs to such as these.'" (Matt. 19. 14)

Jesus loves children, and He adores your baby. God gathers them in His arms and welcomes them with His love. As you prepare for the arrival of your child, remember that God is willing and able to provide for your every need. He will be with you in delivery and He will continue to help you carry out His will. Build your family's life on His firm foundation and trust in His promises. May He give you peace concerning the future and hope to face each day. Your Sovereign Lord loves you and your child forever.

Prayer
Dear Lord,
Thank You for welcoming my child and me into Your arms. Help us to always rest in the safety of Your love. As I await my child's birthday, help me to trust in Your faithfulness. Please give us the perfect peace that comes with knowing You will always be with us in the midst of our struggles. In Jesus' name, amen.

Song
Petra. "I Will Call Upon the Lord." *Petra Praise: The Rock Cries Out.* Word, 1989. CD.

Topical Index

Anger

Week 20 Day 4   p. 128

"…for man's anger does not bring about the righteous life that God desires." (Jas. 1.20)

Week 28 Day 3   p. 179

"But he answered one of them, 'Friend, I am not being unfair to you. Didn't you agree to work for a denarius? Take your pay and go. I want to give the man who was hired last the same as I gave you. Don't I have the right to do what I want with my own money? Or are you envious because I am generous?" (Matt. 20.13-15)

Anxiety

Week 12 Day 1   p. 59

"Cast your cares on the Lord and he will sustain you; he will never let the righteous fall." (Ps. 55.22)

Week 14 Day 2   p. 76

"Humble yourselves therefore, under God's mighty hand, that he may lift you up in due time. Cast all your anxiety on him because he cares for you." (1 Pet. 5.6-7)

Week 33 Day 2   p. 205

"But seek first his kingdom and his righteousness, and all these things will be given to you as well. Therefore do not worry about tomorrow, for tomorrow will worry about itself. Each day has enough trouble of its own." (Matt. 6.33-34)

Bed Rest

Week 17 Day 1   p. 101
"She watches over the affairs of her household and does not
eat the bread of idleness." (Prov. 31.27)

Week 17 Day 4   p. 104
"His master replied, `Well done, good and faithful servant!
You have been faithful with a few things, I will put you in
charge of many things. Come and share your master's
happiness...'" (Matt. 25.21)

Week 24 Day 5   p. 156
"Then, because so many people were coming and going that
they did not even have a chance to eat, he (Jesus) said to them,
"Come with me by yourselves to a quiet place and get some
rest." (Mark 6.31)

Week 26 Day 5   p. 168
"Teach us to number our days aright, that we may gain a
heart of wisdom." (Ps. 90.12)

Week 28 Day 2   p. 178
"Therefore my heart is glad and my tongue rejoices; my body
also will rest secure, because you will not abandon me to the
grave, nor will you let your Holy One see decay. You have
made known to me the path of life; you will fill me with joy in
your presence." (Ps. 16.9-11)

Week 35 Day 2   p. 225
"Unless the Lord builds the house, its builders labor in vain.
Unless the Lord watches over the city, the watchmen stand

guard in vain. In vain you rise early and stay up late, toiling for food to eat-for he grants sleep to those he loves." (Ps. 127.1-2)

Blessing

Week 6 Day 3   p. 12

"Sons are a heritage from the Lord, children a reward from him. Like arrows in the hands of a warrior are sons born in one's youth. Blessed is the man whose quiver is full of them." (Ps.127.3-5)

Week 10 Day 5   p. 48

Restore us, O God; make your face shine upon us, that we may be saved." (Ps. 80.3)

Courage

Week 18 Day 3   p. 112

"...because God has said, "Never will I leave you; never will I forsake you." So we say with confidence, "The Lord is my helper; I will not be afraid. What can man do to me?"" (Heb. 13.5-6)

Week 18 Day 4   p. 113

"Let us fix our eyes on Jesus, the author and perfecter of our faith, who for the joy set before him endured the cross, scorning its shame, and sat down at the right hand of the throne of God. Consider him who endured such opposition from sinful men, so that you will not grow weary and lose heart." (Heb. 12.2-3)

Week 25 Day 3   p. 160
"In addition to all this, take up the shield of faith, with which you can extinguish all the flaming arrows of the evil one." (Eph. 6.15)

Week 25 Day 4 & 5 p. 161-162
"Take the helmet of salvation and the sword of the Spirit, which is the word of God." (Eph. 6.17)

Week 32 Day 5   p. 208
"Have I not commanded you? Be strong and courageous. Do not be terrified; do not be discouraged, for the Lord your God will be with you wherever you go." (Josh. 1.9)

Week 37 Day 5   p. 245
"Blessed is the man who perseveres under trial, because when he has stood the test, he will receive the crown of life that God has promised those who love him." (Jas. 1.12)

Creation

Week 7 Day 5   p. 26
"Before I formed you in the womb I knew you, before you were born I set you apart…" (Jer. 1.5)

Week 11 Day 3   p. 52
"Even the sparrow has found a home, and the swallow a nest for herself, where she may have her young-a place near your altar, O Lord Almighty, my King and my God. Blessed are those who dwell in your house; they are ever praising you. Blessed are those whose strength is in you, who have set their hearts on pilgrimages. As they pass through the Valley of Baca, they make it a place of springs; the autumn rains also cover it with pools." (Ps. 84.3-6)

Week 13 Day 1   p. 67

"For by him all things were created; things in heaven and on earth, visible and invisible, whether thrones or powers or rulers or authorities; all things were created by him and for him. He is before all things, and in him all things hold together." (Col. 1.16-17)

Week 16 Day 5   p. 98

"He has made everything beautiful in its time. He has also set eternity in the hearts of men; yet they cannot fathom what God has done from beginning to end. I know that there is nothing better for men than to be happy and do good while they live. That everyone may eat and drink, and find satisfaction in all his toil-this is the gift of God." (Eccles. 3.11-13)

Week 18 Day 1   p. 109

"I praise you because I am fearfully and wonderfully made; your works are wonderful, I know that full well. My frame was not hidden from you when I was made in the secret place. When I was woven together in the depths of the earth, your eyes saw my unformed body. All the days ordained for me were written in your book before one of them came to be. How precious to me are your thoughts, O god! How vast is the sum of them!" (Ps. 139.14-17)

Week 20 Day 5   p. 136

"For everything God created is good, and nothing is to be rejected if it is received with thanksgiving because it is consecrated by the word of God and prayer." (1 Tim. 4.14)

Week 21 Day 2   p. 134
"Know that the Lord is God. It is he who made us and we are his; we are his people, the sheep of his pasture." (Ps.100.3)

Week 21 Day 5   p. 137
"When I consider your heavens, the work of your fingers, the moon and the stars, which you have set in place, what is man that you are mindful of him, the son of man that you care for him?" (Ps. 8.3-4)

Week 23 Day 3   p. 148
"As you do not know the path of the wind, or how the body is formed in a mother's womb, so you cannot understand the work of God, the Maker of all things." (Eccles. 11.5)

Week 23 Day 4   p. 149
"My frame was not hidden from you when I was made in the secret place. When I was woven together in the depths of the earth, your eyes saw my unformed body. All the days ordained for me were written in your book before one of them came to be." (Ps.139.15-16)

Week 24 Day 1   p. 152
"For since the creation of the world God's invisible qualities-his eternal power and divine nature-have been clearly seen, being understood from what has been made, so that men are without excuse." (Rom.1.20)

Week 29 Day 4   p. 187
"For we are God's workmanship, created in Christ Jesus to do good works, which God prepared in advance for us to do." (Eph. 2.10)

Week 30 Day 1   p. 190
"Do you know when the mountain goats give birth? Do you watch when the doe bears her fawn? Do you count the months till they bear? Do you know the time they give birth? They crouch down and bring forth their young; their labor pains are ended. Their young thrive and grow strong…" (Job 39.1-4)

Week 31 Day 4   p. 201
"For by him all things were created: things in heaven and on earth, visible and invisible, whether thrones or powers or rulers or authorities; all things were created by him and for him. He is before all things, and in him all things hold together." (Col. 1.16-17)

Fear

Week 11 Day 2   p. 51
"Then I said to you, "Do not be terrified; do not be afraid of them. The Lord your God, who is going before you, will fight for you, as he did for you in Egypt, before your very eyes, and in the desert. There you saw how the Lord your God carried you, as a father carries his son, all the way you went until you reached this place." (Deut. 1.29-31)

Week 15 Day 2   p. 84
"I sought the Lord, and he answered me; he delivered me from all my fears." (Ps. 34.4)

Week 15 Day 5   p. 89
"Do not be afraid or terrified because of them, for the Lord your God goes with you; he will never leave you nor forsake you…do not be discouraged." (Deut. 31.6-8)

Week 16 Day 4   p. 96
"But Jesus immediately said to them: "Take courage! It is I. Don't be afraid." "Lord, if it's you," Peter replied, "tell me to come to you on the water." "Come," he said." (Matt. 14.27-29)

Week 19 Day 1   p. 117
"But now, this is what the Lord says-he who created you, O Jacob, he who formed you, O Israel: "Fear not, for I have redeemed you; I have summoned you by name; you are mine. When you pass through the waters, I will be with you; and when you pass through the rivers, they will not sweep over you. When you walk through the fire, you will not be burned; the flames will not set you ablaze. For I am the Lord, your God, the Holy One of Israel, your Savior; I give Egypt for your ransom, Cush and Seba in your stead. Since you are precious and honored in my sight, and because I love you, I will give men in exchange for you, and people in exchange for your life. Do not be afraid, for I am with you…" (Isa. 43.1-5)

Week 19 Day 4   p. 120
"…Do not be fainthearted or afraid; do not be terrified or give way to panic before them. For the Lord your God is the one who goes with you to fight for you against your enemies to give you victory." (Deut. 20.3-4)

Week 24 Day 3   p. 154
"Surely he will never by shaken; a righteous man will be remembered forever. He will have no fear of bad news; his heart is steadfast, trusting in the Lord." (Ps.112.6-7)

Week 29 Day 2   p. 185
"Surely God is my salvation; I will trust and not be afraid. The Lord, the Lord, is my strength and my song; he has become my salvation." (Isa. 12.2)

Week 32 Day 1   p. 204
"When I am afraid I will trust in you." (Ps. 56.3)

Week 38 Day 4   p. 251
"God is our refuge and strength, an ever-present help in trouble. Therefore we will not fear, though the earth give way and the mountains fall into the heart of the sea, though its waters roar and foam and the mountains quake with their surging." (Ps. 46.1-2)

Week 40 Day 2   p. 262
"When I am afraid, I will trust in you. In God, whose word I praise, in God I trust; I will not be afraid. What can mortal man do to me?" (Ps. 56.3-4)

Week 40 Day 4   p. 264
"So do not fear, for I am with you; do not be dismayed, for I am your God. I will strengthen you and help you; I will uphold you with my righteous right hand." (Isa. 41.10)

God's Faithfulness
Week 12 Day 3   p. 61
"But if from there you seek the Lord your God you will find him if you look for him with all your heart and with all your soul. When you are in distress and all these things have happened to you, then in later days you will return to the Lord your God and obey him. For the Lord your God is a

merciful God; he will not abandon or destroy you or forget the covenant with your forefathers..." (Deut. 4.29-31)

Week 13 Day 2   p. 68
"Because of your great compassion you did not abandon them in the desert. By day the pillar of cloud did not cease to guide them on their path, nor the pillar of fire by night to shine on the way they were to take. You gave your good Spirit to instruct them. You did not withhold your manna from their mouths, and you gave them water for their thirst. For forty years you sustained them in the desert; they lacked nothing..." (Neh. 9.10-21)

Week 15 Day 3   p. 86
"Blessed is he whose help is the God of Jacob, whose hope is in the Lord his God, the Maker of heaven and earth, the seas, & everything in them-the Lord remains faithful forever." (Ps. 146.5-6)

Week 16 Day 2   p. 93
"Your ways, O God, are holy. What god is so great as our God? You are the God who performs miracles; you display your power among the peoples. With your mighty arm you redeemed your people...Your path led through the sea, your way through the mighty waters, though your footprints were not seen. You led your people like a flock by the hand of Moses and Aaron." (Ps. 77.13-20)

Week 18 Day 5   p. 114
Jesus Calms the Storm
"Then he got into the boat and his disciples followed him. Without warning, a furious storm came up on the lake, so that the waves swept over the boat. But Jesus was sleeping. The

disciples went and woke him, saying, "Lord, save us! We're going to drown!" He replied, "You of little faith, why are you so afraid?" Then he got up and rebuked the winds and the waves, and it was completely calm. The men were amazed and asked, "What kind of man is this? Even the winds and the waves obey him!" (Matt. 8.23-27)

Week 27 Day 2   p. 172
"He tends his flock like a shepherd; He gathers the lambs in his arms and carries them close to his heart; he gently leads those that have young." (Isa. 40.11)

Week 27 Day 3   p. 173
"The Lord is my rock, my fortress and my deliverer; my God is my rock, in whom I take refuge. He is my shield and the horn of my salvation, my stronghold." (Ps. 18.2)

Week 34 Day 2   p. 218
"Are not five sparrows sold for two pennies? Yet not one of them is forgotten by God. Indeed, the very hairs of your head are all numbered. Don't be afraid; you are worth more than many sparrows." (Luke 12.6-7)

Week 34 Day 5   p. 222
"The Lord is righteous in all his ways and loving toward all he has made. The Lord is near to all who call on him, to all who call on him in truth. He fulfills the desires of those who fear him; he hears their cry and saves them. The Lord watches over all who love him, but the wicked he will destroy." (Ps. 145.17-20)

Week 36 Day 5   p. 238
"Your kingdom is an everlasting kingdom, and your dominion endures through all generations. The Lord is faithful to all his promises and loving toward all he has made. The Lord upholds all those who fall and lifts up all who are bowed down. The eyes of all look to you, and you give them their food at the proper time. You open your hand and satisfy the desires of every living thing." (Ps. 145.13-15)

Week 39 Day 5   p. 259
"When Jesus saw his mother there, and the disciple whom he loved standing nearby, he said to his mother, "Dear woman, here is your son," and to the disciple, "Here is your mother." From that time on, this disciple took her into his home." (John 19. 26-27)

God's Will

Week 8 Day 5   p. 35
"…Then Eli said, He is the Lord; let him do what is good in his eyes." (1 Sam. 3.18)

Week 9 Day 5   p. 41
"Forget the former things; do not dwell on the past. See, I am doing a new thing! Now it springs up; do you not perceive it? I am making a way in the desert." (Isa. 43.18-19)

Week 16 Day 1   p. 92
"Father, if you are willing, take this cup from me; yet not my will, but yours be done." (Luke 22.42)

Week 20 Day 2   p. 125
"Many are the plans in a man's heart, but it is the Lord's purpose that prevails." (Prov. 19.21)

Week 20 Day 3   p. 126
"As he went along, he saw a man blind from birth. His disciples asked him, "Rabbi, who sinned, this man or his parents, that he was born blind?" Neither this man nor his parents sinned," said Jesus, "but this happened so that the work of God might be displayed in his life…so the man went and washed, and came home seeing." (John 9.1-7)

Week 23 Day 2   p. 146
"However, as it is written: "No eye has seen, no ear has heard, no mind has conceived what God has prepared for those who love him"-but God has revealed it to us by his Spirit." (1Cor. 2.9)

Week 29 Day 1   p. 184
"He has made everything beautiful in his time. He has also set eternity in the hearts of men; yet they cannot fathom what God has done from beginning to end." (Eccles. 3.11)

Week 30 Day 2   p. 191
"I know that you can do all things; no plan of yours can be thwarted…Surely I spoke of things I did not understand, things too wonderful for me to know." (Job 42.2)

Week 35 Day 5   p. 230
"Delight yourself in the Lord and he will give you the desires of your heart." (Ps. 37.4)

Heroes of Faith

Week 6 Day 4   p. 15

"The angel went to her and said, "Greetings, you who are highly favored! The Lord is with you." Mary was greatly troubled at his words and wondered what kind of greeting this might be. But the angel said to her, "Do not be afraid, Mary, you have found favor with God. You will be with child and give birth to a son, and you are to give him the name Jesus…" I am the Lord's servant," Mary answered. "May it be to me as you have said." Then the angel left her."
(Luke 1.28-38)

Week 7 Day 2   p. 22

"Sarah said, "God has brought me laughter, and everyone who hears about this will laugh with me." And she added, "Who would have said to Abraham that Sarah would nurse children? Yet I have borne him a son in his old age."
(Gen. 21.6)

Week 7 Day 3   p. 23

"Now the Lord was gracious to Sarah as he had said, and the Lord did for Sarah what he had promised. Sarah became pregnant and bore a son to Abraham in his old age, at the very time God had promised him." (Gen. 21.1-2)

Week 7 Day 4   p. 25

"Sarah said, "God has brought me laughter, and everyone who hears about this will laugh with me." (Gen. 21.6)

Week 8 Day 1   p. 28

"He settles the barren woman in her home as a happy mother of children. Praise the Lord." (Ps. 113.9)

Week 8 Day 2   p. 29
"And the Lord was gracious to Hannah; she conceived and
gave birth to three sons and two daughters. Meanwhile, the
boy Samuel grew up in the presence of the Lord."
(1 Sam. 2.21)

Week 8 Day 3   p. 30
"I prayed for this child, and the Lord has granted me what I
asked of him. So now I give him to the Lord. For his whole
life he will be given over to the Lord." And he worshiped the
Lord there." (1 Sam. 1.27)

Week 8 Day 4   p. 33
"Each year his mother made him a little robe and took it to
him when she went up with her husband to offer the annual
sacrifice. Eli would bless Elkanah and his wife, saying, "May
the Lord give you children by this woman to take the place of
the one she prayed for and gave to the Lord." Then they
would go home. And the Lord was gracious to Hannah; she
conceived and gave birth to three sons and two daughters.
Meanwhile, the boy Samuel grew up in the presence of the
Lord." (1 Sam. 2.19-21)

Week 9 Day 2   p. 38
"Now when Daniel learned that the decree had been
published, he went home to his upstairs room where the
windows opened toward Jerusalem. Three times a day he got
down on his knees and prayed, giving thanks to his God, just
as he had done before. Then these men went as a group and
found Daniel praying and asking God for help. So they went
to the king and spoke to him about his royal decree..."
(Dan. 6.10-12)

Week 9 Day 3   p. 39
"So the king gave the order, and they brought Daniel and
threw him into the lions' den. The king said to Daniel, "May
your God, whom you serve continually, rescue you!...The king
was over joyed and gave orders to lift Daniel out of the den.
And when Daniel was lifted from the den, no wound was
found on him, because he had trusted in his God."
(Dan. 6.16-22)

Week 9 Day 4   p. 40
"Then King Darius wrote to all the peoples, nations and men
of every language throughout the land: "May you prosper
greatly! "I issue a decree that in every part of my kingdom
people must fear and reverence the God of Daniel. "For he is
the living God and he endures forever; his kingdom will not
be destroyed, his dominion will never end. He rescues and he
saves; he performs signs and wonders in the heavens and on
the earth. He has rescued Daniel from the power of the lions."
(Dan. 6.25-27)

Week 11 Day 1   p. 50
"By faith Abraham, when God tested him, offered Isaac as a
sacrifice. He who had received the promises was about to
sacrifice his one and only son, even though God had said to
him, "It is through Isaac that your offspring will be reckoned."
Abraham reasoned that God could raise the dead, and
figuratively speaking, he did receive Isaac back from death."
(Heb. 11.17-19)

Week 11 Day 4   p. 54
"Isaac prayed to the Lord on behalf of his wife, because she
was barren. The Lord answered his prayer, and his wife
Rebekah became pregnant. The babies jostled each other

within her, and she said, "Why is this happening to me?" So she went to inquire of the Lord. The Lord said to her, "Two nations are in your womb, and two peoples from within you will be separated; one people will be stronger than the other, and the older will serve the younger." (Gen. 25.21-23)

Week 14 Day 5   p. 80
"...Do not think that because you are in the king's house you alone of all the Jews will escape. For if you remain silent at this time, relief and deliverance for the Jews will arise from another place, but you and your father's family will perish. And who knows but that you have come to royal position for such a time as this?" (Esth. 4.12-14)

Week 31 Day 1   p. 197
"Furious with rage, Nebuchadnezzar summoned Shadrach, Meshach and Abednego. So these men were brought before the king, and Nebuchadnezzar said to them, "Is it true, Shadrach, Meshach and Abednego, that you do not serve my gods or worship the image of gold I have set up? Now when you hear the sound of the horn, flute, zither, lyre, harp, pipes and all kind of music, if you are ready to fall down and worship the image I made, very good. But if you do not worship it, you will be thrown immediately into a blazing furnace. Then what god will be able to rescue you from my hand?" (Dan. 3.13-15)

Week 31 Day 2   p. 198
"Shadrach, Meshach and Abednego replied to the king, "O Nebuchadnezzar, we do not need to defend ourselves before you in this matter. If we are thrown into the blazing furnace, the God we serve is able to save us from it, and he will rescue us from your hand, O king. But even if he does not, we want

you to know, O king, that we will not serve your gods or worship the image of gold you have set up." (Dan. 3.16-19)

Week 31 Day 3   p. 199

"The king's command was so urgent and the furnace so hot that the flames of the fire killed the soldiers who took up Shadrach, Meshach and Abednego, and these three men, firmly tied, fell into the blazing furnace. Then King Nebuchadnezzar leaped to his feet in amazement and asked his advisers, "Weren't there three men that we tied up and threw into the fire?...Then Nebuchadnezzar said, "Praise be to the God of Shadrach, Meshach and Abednego, who has sent his angel and rescued his servants! They trusted in him and defied the king's command and were willing to give up their lives rather than serve or worship any god except their own God. Therefore I decree that the people of any nation or language who say anything against the God of Shadrach, Meshach and Abednego be cut into pieces and their houses be turned into piles of rubble, for no other god can save in this way." (Dan. 3.22-29)

Week 38 Day 5   p. 252

The Healing of a Boy With a Demon

"When they came to the crowd, a man approached Jesus and knelt before him. Lord, but have mercy on my son," he said. "He has seizures and is suffering greatly. He often falls into the fire or into the water. I brought him to your disciples, but they could not heal him."

"O unbelieving and perverse generation," Jesus replied, "how long shall I stay with you? How long shall I put up with you? Bring the boy here to me." Jesus rebuked the demon, and it came out of the boy, and he was healed from that moment. Then the disciples came to Jesus in private and asked, "Why couldn't we drive it out?" He replied, "Because you have so little faith. I tell you the truth, if you have faith as small as a mustard seed, you can say to this mountain, 'Move from here to there' and it will move. Nothing will be impossible for you." (Matt. 17.14-20)

Hope

Week 12 Day 4   p. 63
"The Lord delights in those who fear him, who put their hope in his unfailing love." (Ps. 147.11)

Week 12 Day 5   p. 64
"I wait for the Lord, my soul waits, and in his word I put my hope." (Ps. 130.5)

Week 17 Day 2   p. 102
"Why are you downcast, O my soul? Why so disturbed within me? Put your hope in God, for I will yet praise him, my Savior & my God." (Ps. 42.5)

Week 20 Day 1   p. 124
"So we fix our eyes not on what is seen, but on what is unseen. For what is seen is temporary, but what is unseen is eternal." (2 Cor. 4.18)

Week 21 Day 1   p. 132
"But we have this treasure in jars of clay to show that this all surpassing power is from God and not from us. We are hard pressed on every side, but not crushed, perplexed, but not in despair; persecuted, but not abandoned; struck down, but not destroyed." (2 Cor. 4.7-9)

Week 24 Day 4   p. 155
"The Lord delights in those who fear him, who put their hope in his unfailing love." (Ps. 147.11)

Week 28 Day 4   p. 181
"Now faith is being sure of what we hope for and certain of what we do not see." (Heb. 11:1)

Week 29 Day 3   p. 186
"We wait in hope for the Lord; he is our help and our shield. In him our hearts rejoice, for we trust in his holy name. May your unfailing love rest upon us, O Lord, even as we put our hope in you." (Ps. 33.20-22)

Week 33 Day 1   p. 210
"Find rest, O my soul in God alone; my hope comes from him. He alone is my rock and my salvation; he is my fortress, I will not be shaken." (Ps. 62.5)

Week 40 Day 3   p. 263
"We wait in hope for the Lord; he is our help and our shield. In him our hearts rejoice, for we trust in his holy name. May your unfailing love rest upon us, O Lord, even as we put our hope in you." (Ps. 33.20-22)

Patience

Week 21 Day 3   p. 135
"Consider it pure joy, my brothers, whenever you face trials of many kinds, because you know that the testing of your faith develops perseverance. Perseverance must finish its work so that you may be mature and complete, not lacking anything..." (Jas. 1.2-4) "...blessed is the man who perseveres under trial, because when he has stood the test, he will receive

the crown of life that God has promised to those who love him." (Jas. 1.12)

Week 36 Day 1   p. 232

"My soul is in anguish. How long, O Lord, how long? Turn, O Lord, and deliver me; save me because of your unfailing love…I am worn out from groaning; all night long I flood my bed with weeping and drench my couch with tears. My eyes grow weak with sorrow…The Lord has heard my cry for mercy; the Lord accepts my prayer." (Ps. 6.3-9)

Week 37 Day 3   p. 242

"There is a time for everything, and a season for every activity under heaven: a time to be born…He has made everything beautiful in its time. He has also set eternity in the hearts of men; yet they cannot fathom what God has done from beginning to end." (Eccles. 3:1-11)

Peace

Week 19 Day 5   p. 122

"Peace I leave with you; my peace I give you. I do not give to you as the world gives. Do not let your hearts be troubled and do not be afraid." (John 14.27)

Week 23 Day 1   p. 145

"May the God of peace, who through the blood of the eternal covenant brought back from the dead our Lord Jesus, that great Shepherd of the sheep, equip you with everything good for doing his will, and may he work in us what is pleasing to him, through Jesus Christ, to whom be glory for ever and ever. Amen." (Heb.13.20)

Week 25 Day 2   p. 159
"Stand firm then, with the belt of truth buckled around your waist, with the breastplate of righteousness in place, and with your feet fitted with the readiness that comes from the gospel of peace." (Eph. 6.14-15)

Week 35 Day 3   p. 227
"A heart at peace gives life to the body, but envy rots the bones." (Prov. 15.13)

Week 40 Day 1   p. 261
"You will keep in perfect peace him whose mind is steadfast, because he trusts in you. Trust in the Lord forever, for the Lord, the Lord, is the Rock eternal." (Isa. 26.3-4)

Week 40 Day 5   p. 265
You will keep in perfect peace him whose mind is steadfast, because he trusts in you. Trust in the Lord forever for the Lord, the Lord, is the Rock eternal." (Isa. 26.3-4)

Praise
Week 6 Day 5   p. 16
"Come and see what God has done, how awesome his works in man's behalf." (Ps. 66.5)

Week 9 Day 1   p. 37
"You turned my wailing into dancing; you removed my sackcloth and clothed me with joy, my heart may sing to you and not be silent. O my god, I will give you thanks forever." (Ps. 30.11-12)

Week 10 Day 1   p. 43
"This is the day the Lord has made; let us rejoice and be glad in it." (Ps. 118.24)

Week 15 Day 4   p. 87
"Now to him who is able to do immeasurably more than all we ask or imagine according to his power that is at work within us, to him be glory in the church and in Christ Jesus throughout all generations, for ever and ever! Amen." (Eph. 3.20)

Week 21 Day 4   p. 136
"Let them praise his name with dancing and make music to him with tambourine and harp. For the Lord takes delight in his people; he crowns the humble with salvation." (Ps. 149.3-4)

Week 24 Day 2   p. 153
"And they sang a new song: "You are worthy to take the scroll and to open its seals, because you were slain, and with your blood you purchased men for God from every tribe and language and people and nation." (Rev. 5.9)

Week 26 Day 4   p. 167
"I have told you this so that my joy may be in you and that your joy may be complete. My command is this: Love each other as I have loved you. Greater love has no one than this, that he lay down his life for his friends." (John 15.11-13)

Week 32 Day 2   p. 205
"Be my rock of refuge, to which I can always go; give the command to save me, for you are my rock and fortress…From

birth, I have relied on you; you brought me forth from my mother's womb. I will ever praise you." (Ps. 71.3-6)

Week 36 Day 2   p. 234
"I will exalt you, my God the King; I will praise your name forever and ever. Every day I will praise you and extol your name for ever and ever." (Ps.145.1-2)

Prayer

Week 13 Day 5   p. 72
"What other nation is so great as to have their gods near them the way the Lord our God is near us whenever we pray to him?" (Deut. 4.7)

Week 26 Day 1   p. 164
"And pray in the Spirit on all occasions with all kinds of prayers and requests. With this in mind, be alert and always keep on praying for all the saints." (Eph. 6.18)

Week 26 Day 3   p. 166
"If you remain in me and my words remain in you, ask whatever you wish, and it will be given you. This is to my Father's glory, that you bear much fruit, showing yourselves to be my disciples. "As the Father has loved me, so have I loved you. Now remain in my love." (John 15.7-9)

Week 30 Day 3   p. 192
"...The Lord is near. Do not be anxious about anything, but in everything, by prayer and petition, with thanksgiving present your requests to God. And the peace of God, which transcends all understanding will guard your hearts and your minds in Christ Jesus." (Phil. 4.4-7)

Week 31 Day 5   p. 202
"If you remain in me and my words remain in you, ask whatever you wish, and it will be given you." (John 15.7)

Week 32 Day 3   p. 206
"Be joyful in hope, patient in affliction, faithful in prayer." (Rom. 12.12)

Week 37 Day 4   p. 243
"For this reason, since the day we heard about you, we have not stopped praying for you and asking God to fill you with the knowledge of his will through all spiritual wisdom and understanding...being strengthened with all power according to his glorious might so that you may have great endurance and patience, and joyfully giving thanks to the Father, who has qualified you to share in the inheritance of the saints in the kingdom of light." (Col. 1.9-12)

Week 38 Day 3   p. 251
"You may ask me for anything in my name, and I will do it." (John 14.14)

Week 39 Day 4   p. 258
"What other nation is so great as to have their gods near them the way the Lord our God is near us whenever we pray to him?" (Deut. 4.7)

Strength
Week 15 Day 1   p. 83
"How lovely is your dwelling place, O Lord Almighty! My soul yearns, even faints, for the courts of the Lord; my heart and my flesh cry out for the living God. Even the sparrow has found a home, and the swallow a nest for herself, where she

may have her young-a place near your altar, O Lord Almighty, my King and my God. Blessed are those who dwell in your house; they are ever praising you. Blessed are those whose strength is in you, who have set their hearts on pilgrimage." (Ps. 84.1-5)

Week 17 Day 3   p. 104
"Do you not know? Have you not heard? The Lord is the everlasting God, the Creator of the ends of the earth. He will not grow tired or weary, and his understanding no one can fathom. He gives strength to the weary and increases the power of the weak. Even youths grow tired and weary, and young men stumble and fall; but those who hope in the Lord will renew their strength. They will soar on wings like eagles; they will run and not grow weary, they will walk and not be faint." (Isa. 40.28-31)

Week 18 Day 2   p. 111
"God is our refuge and strength, an ever-present help in trouble. Therefore we will not fear, though the earth give way and the mountains fall into the heart of the sea, though its waters roar and foam and the mountains quake with their surging." (Ps. 46.1-2)

Week 22 Day 2   p. 140
"Turn to me and have mercy on me; grant your strength to your servant and save the son of your maidservant." (Ps. 86.16)

Week 25 Day 1 p. 158
"Finally, be strong in the Lord and in his mighty power. Put on the full armor of God so that you can take your stand against the devil's schemes." (Eph. 6.10)

Week 26 Day 1   p. 164
"Finally, be strong in the Lord and in his mighty power. Put on the full armor of God so that you can take your stand against the devil's schemes." (Eph. 6.10)

Week 27 Day 4   p. 174
"Nehemiah said, "Go and enjoy choice food and sweet drinks, and send some to those who have nothing prepared. This day is sacred to our Lord. Do not grieve, for the joy of the Lord is your strength." (Neh. 8.10)

Week 28 Day 1   p. 177
"Finally, be strong in the Lord and in his mighty power."
(Eph. 6.10)

Week 35 Day 3   p. 226
"The Lord gives strength to his people; the Lord blesses his people with peace."
(Ps. 29.11)

Week 38 Day 1   p. 241
"Blessed are those whose strength is in you, who have set their hearts on pilgrimage." (Ps. 84.5)

Week 38 Day 2   p. 248
"Lift your eyes and look to the heavens; Who created all these? He who brings out the starry host one by one, and calls them each by name. Because of his great power and mighty

strength, not one of them is missing. Why do you say, O Jacob, and complain, O Israel, "My way is hidden from the Lord; my cause is disregarded by my God"? Do you not know? Have you not heard? The Lord is the everlasting God, the Creator of the ends of the earth. He will not grow tired or weary, and his understanding no one can fathom. He gives strength to the weary and increases the power of the weak. Even youths grow tired and weary, and young men stumble and fall; but those who hope in the Lord will renew their strength. They will soar on wings like eagles; they will run and not grow weary, they will walk and not be faint."
(Isa. 40.26-31)

Suffering
Week 9 Day 1   p. 37
"You turned my wailing into dancing; you removed my sackcloth and clothed me with joy, my heart may sing to you and not be silent. O my god, I will give you thanks forever."
(Ps. 30.11-12)

Week 36 Day 3   p. 235
"I consider that our present sufferings are not worth comparing with the glory that will be revealed in us. The creation waits in eager expectation for the sons of God to be revealed. For the creation was subjected to frustration, not by its own choice, but by the will of the one who subjected it, in hope that the creation itself will be liberated from its bondage to decay and brought into the glorious freedom of the children of God. We know that the whole creation has been groaning as in the pains of childbirth right up to the present time. Not only so, but we ourselves, who have the firstfruits of the Spirit, groan inwardly as we wait eagerly for our adoption as

sons, the redemption of our bodies. For in this hope we were saved. But hope that is seen is no hope at all. Who hopes for what he already has? But if we hope for what we do not yet have, we wait for it patiently." (Rom. 8.18-25)

Week 37 Day 1   p. 240
"Then he said to them, "My soul is overwhelmed with sorrow to the point of death. Stay here and keep watch with me." Going a little farther, he fell with his face to the ground and prayed, "My Father, if it is possible, may this cup be taken from me. Yet not as I will, but as you will." (Matt. 26.38-39)

Week 37 Day 2   p. 241
"A bruised reed he will not break, and a smoldering wick he will not snuff out, till he leads justice to victory. In his name the nations will put that hope." (Matt.12.20-21)

Week 40 Day 4   p. 264
"A woman giving birth to a child has pain because her time has come; but when her baby is born she forgets the anguish because of her joy that a child is born into the world." (John 16.21)

Thanksgiving
Week 22 Day 3   p. 141
"I thank my God every time I remember you. In all my prayers for all of you, I always pray with joy because of your partnership in the gospel from the first day until now, being confident of this, that he who began a good work in you will carry it on to completion until the day of Christ Jesus." (Phil. 1.3-6)

Week 22 Day 4   p. 142
"Give thanks to the Lord, for he is good; his love endures forever." (1 Chron. 16.34)

Tired and Weary

Week 27 Day 1   p. 171
"Do you not know? Have you not heard? The Lord is the everlasting God, the Creator of the ends of the earth. He will not grow tired or weary, and his understanding no one can fathom. He gives strength to the weary and increases the power of the weak. Even youths grow tired and weary, and young men stumble and fall; but those who hope in the Lord will renew their strength. They will soar on wings like eagles; they will run and not grow weary, they will walk and not be faint." (Isa. 40.28-31)

Week 32 Day 4   p. 207
"When you lie down, you will not be afraid; when you lie down, your sleep will be sweet." (Prov. 3.24)

Week 34 Day 3   p. 219
"Come to me, all you who are weary and burdened, and I will give you rest." (Matt. 11.28)

Trust

Week 6 Day 1   p. 9
"Look to the Lord and his strength; seek his face always." (1 Chron. 16.11)

Week 11 Day 5   p. 56
"Do not let your hearts be troubled. Trust in God; trust also in me. In my Father's house are many rooms; if it were not so, I

would not have told you. And if I go and prepare a place for you, I will come back and take you to be with me that you also may be where I am. You know the way to the place I am going." (John 14.1-4)

Week 16 Day 3   p. 95
"Trust in the Lord with all your heart and lean not on your own understanding; in all your ways acknowledge him, and he will make your paths straight." (Prov. 3.5-6)

Week 33 Day 4   p. 214
"To you, O Lord, I lift up my soul; in you I trust, O my God." (Ps. 25.1)

Week 34 Day 1   p. 217
"I waited patiently for the Lord; he turned to me and heard my cry. He lifted me out of the slimy pit, out of the mud and mire; he set my feet on a rock and gave me a firm place to stand. He put a new song in my mouth, a hymn of praise to our God. Many will see and fear and put their trust in the Lord. Blessed is the man who makes the Lord his trust, who does not look to the proud, to those who turn aside to false gods. Many, O Lord my God, are the wonders you have done. The things you planned for us no one can recount to you; were I to speak and tell of them, they would be too many to declare." (Ps. 40.1-5)

Week 39 Day 1   p. 255
"He who dwells in the shelter of the Most High will rest in the shadow of the Almighty. I will say of the Lord, "He is my refuge and my fortress, my God, in whom I trust.""
(Ps. 91.1-2)

Wonders of God

Week 6 Day 2   p. 11
"Remember the wonders he has done, his miracles, and the judgments he pronounced..." (1 Chron.16.10-13)

Week 7 Day 1   p. 20
"Are not two sparrows sold for a penny? Yet not one of them will fall to the ground apart from the will of your Father. And even the very hairs of your head are all numbered. So don't be afraid; you are worth more than many sparrows."
(Matt. 10.29-30)

Week 29 Day 5   p. 188
"I will consider all your works and meditate on all your mighty deeds." Your ways, God, are holy. What god is as great as our God? You are the God who performs miracles; you display your power among the peoples. With your mighty arm you redeemed your people, the descendants of Jacob and Joseph." (Ps. 77.12-15)

Week 35 Day 4   p. 228
"Then I thought, "To this I will appeal; the years when the Most High stretched out his right hand. I will remember the deeds of the Lord; yes, I will remember your miracles of long ago."" (Ps. 77.10-11)

Week 36 Day 4   p. 237
"Great is the Lord and most worthy of praise; his greatness no one can fathom. The generation will commend your works to another; they will tell of your mighty acts. They will speak of the glorious splendor of your majesty, and I will meditate on your works. They will tell of the power of your awesome works, and I will proclaim your great deeds." (Ps. 145.3-6)

WORKS CITED

American College of Obstetricians and Gynecologists. *Prenatal Development: How Your Baby Grows During Pregnancy.* acog.org. Web, 21 Apr. 2016.

Hallesby, O. "Lina Sandell." Prayer. Fortress Press, 1994. 147. Print.

Hoerber, Robert G. Concordia Self-study Bible: New International Version. St. Louis: Concordia Pub. House, 1986. Print.

Hughey, Billy, and Janice Hughey. *A Rainbow of Hope: 777 Inspirational Quotes plus Selected Scriptures.* El Reno, Oka.: Rainbow Studies, 1994. Print.

Karpenko, Bill. ed. *In Thy Light We See Light Lucem the Valparaiso University Prayer Book.* Valpraiso University, 2008. 9. Print.

Ladd, Karol. The Power of a Positive Mom. West Monroe, LA: Howard, 2001. Print.

Lowdermilk, Deitra, and Shannon Perry. *Maternity & Women's Health Care. 8th ed.* Philadelphia, 2004. Print

Pincott, Jena. *Mom Candy: 1,000 Quotes of Inspiration for Mothers.* Random House, 2012. 135. Print.

U.S. National Library of Medicine. Medline Plus. *Fetal Development.* nlm.nih.gov. Web, 21 Apr. 2016.

Ylvasiker, John. "Borning Cry." *Evangelical Hymnal.* Minneapolis, MN: Augsburg Fortress Press, 2006. Print.

Zacharias, Ravi K. *The Grand Weaver: How God Shapes Us through the Events of Our Lives.* Grand Rapids, MI: Zondervan, 2007. Print.
---. *I, Isaac, Take Thee, Rebekah: Moving from Romance to Lasting Love.* Nashville, TN: W Pub. Group, 2004. 39. Print.

---. *Recapture the Wonder.* Nashville: Integrity, 2003. 47. Print.

ABOUT THE AUTHOR

Sandy Collins is a registered nurse with first-hand experience with high-risk pregnancy. She lives in Georgia with her husband and four children.
Email Sandy at **pregnancydevotions@outlook.com.**

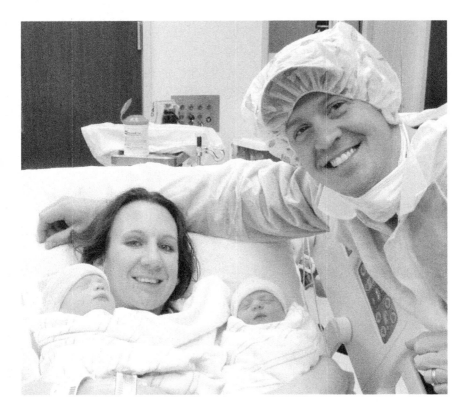

Made in the USA
Las Vegas, NV
21 December 2023

83396890R00167